AI & Data Literacy

Empowering Citizens of Data Science

Bill Schmarzo

BIRMINGHAM—MUMBAI

AI & Data Literacy

Lead Senior Publishing Product Manager: Tushar Gupta

Project Editor: Janice Gonsalves

Content Development Editor: Tanya D'cruz

Copy Editor: Safis Editing

Technical Editor: Aniket Shetty

Proofreader: Safis Editing

Indexer: Sejal Dsilva

Presentation Designer: Pranit Padwal

Developer Relations Marketing Executive: Monika Sangwan

First published: July 2023

Production reference: 1190723

Published by Packt Publishing Ltd.
Grosvenor House
11 St Paul's Square
Birmingham
B3 1RB, UK.

ISBN 978-1-83508-350-5

www.packt.com

Endorsements

Generative AI has burst onto the scene with great promise and huge hype, and has caused significant concern. Bill's pragmatic and clear approach to explaining how AI works, what it can and cannot do, and how people are actually in control of the way models work and produce results is a much-needed treatment of the topic. I always look to Bill for an accessible assessment of new technologies and trends. In this book on AI, Bill has delivered an overview and explanation that will put many at ease in their newly found understanding of AI.

—John Thompson, EY, Global Head of AI

Whether you are just starting to explore AI or are a seasoned data scientist looking to power up to the next value level for your enterprise, Schmarzo provides a clear yet efficacious framework to allow you to comprehend, wrestle with, and most importantly, apply AI to unlock its full potential, empowering better decisions for your business. Schmarzo has the rare gift of blending cutting-edge academic research with real-world experience, making him a gifted educator who makes technical concepts accessible and easy to apply to any sector or enterprise. If you are worried the big data revolution will leave you behind, this book shows you exactly how to become a Citizen of Data Science and make AI a tool that works for you.

—David Hayes, President Coe College

Bill Schmarzo's latest book is a masterful guide for those looking to build their knowledge and literacy at the intersection of data science and AI. With a clear and concise educational framework, Schmarzo guides readers through everything from data privacy and analytics literacy to decision-making and the ethics of AI. This book is an essential read for anyone looking to become a proficient Citizen of Data Science.

—Doug Laney, author of Infonomics and Data Juice

The emergence of ChatGPT has brought a lot of excitement, caution, and suspicion toward AI and data science. This is a momentous opportunity to educate the public on the methods, assumptions, benefits, and risks behind this elusive technology. Bill Schmarzo's book, AI & Data Literacy, is an important work to help society understand AI's business, environmental, social, and economic potential. Bill's ability to relate complex subjects using intuitive explanations sets him apart among the field experts. In addition, his generosity and commitment to share such valuable insights for the benefit of the community is truly inspiring. Bill is a true role model for aspiring data leaders and educators everywhere.

—David Hendrawirawan, Founder, Data Integrity First

Bill's book on AI and data literacy is a very timely read. With everyone talking about AI replacing almost everything we do, it's important to be grounded in the fundamentals of AI, data, and how the combination of the two helps us make better personal and professional decisions. The book covers the basics, the in-depth, and the key understandings needed to navigate the conversation today and into the future.

—Howard Miller, CIO at UCLA Anderson School of Management

Mr. Bill Schmarzo's expertise in data science and artificial intelligence is unmatched, and his passion for sharing knowledge is truly inspiring. Through this book, he demonstrates his unwavering commitment to empowering individuals with the necessary skills and insights to navigate the complex world of data. I wholeheartedly recommend AI & Data Literacy: Empowering Citizens of Data Science to anyone seeking to expand their understanding of data science and its impact on our world. Bill Schmarzo's expertise, passion, and genuine desire to help others make this book an invaluable resource that will undoubtedly shape the future of data literacy.

—Dr. Mouwafac Sidaoui, Chief Academic Officer and Dean of School of Business, Menlo College

From chatbots and virtual assistants to self-driving cars and predictive sales analytics, AI is changing people's lives. More than ever, it is imperative for individuals and organizations to understand what it means to become AI and data literate. It is now a requirement to be a Citizen of Data Science to stay competitive, make ethical decisions, and protect data and privacy. This book empowers us to become a Citizen of Data Science with sensibility, humor, and relatable stories, all the while reminding us of our obligation to be better humans.

—Renée B. Lahti, Chief Innovation Officer, Board Advisor & Continuous Learner

Bill Schmarzo is an educator at heart. For the last several decades, he's focused on lifting the data competency and design thinking literacy of thousands via his various platforms, including teaching and guest lecturing at a number of colleges and universities on multiple continents, publishing multiple academic texts, business workbooks, and kids-style cartoons, and fostering one of the most active data communities on LinkedIn. In his latest book, AI & Data Literacy: Empowering Citizens of Data Science, *Bill shifts his focus to the rapidly growing world of artificial intelligence, arguably the most important development in computing since the internet.*

—Jeff Frick, Principal and Founder, Menlo Creek Media, Host of the Work 20XX and Turn the Lens podcasts

I have known Bill for a number of years, during which time he used the concepts from his books in workshops tailored for business decision-makers and lectures for postgraduate students in Ireland. This book further demonstrates Bill's uncanny ability to bridge the chasm between practice and academia. He leverages contemporary academic knowledge and applies it to address complex business challenges encountered by project and management teams that seek to use advanced analytics to create economic value in dynamic business environments. This book will appeal to practitioners keen to continue their professional development, as well as complement executive and postgraduate education programs that challenge their students to grapple with analytical-based decision making and organizational readiness to embed analytical tools and techniques into organizations across all sectors and industries.

—Dr. Denis Dennehy (Ph.D.), Associate Professor, Swansea University, Wales

A must-have book for everyone in the era of artificial intelligence, networks, platforms, and digital ecosystems.

—Gregory D Esau, SmartSwarms Performance Digital Ecosystems

Get ready to stamp your data passport, since the Dean of Big Data is on a mission to be convert us all to Citizens of Data Science. As only an educator, thought leader, and natural storyteller can, Bill Schmarzo adeptly highlights how individuals and corporations alike can leverage the power of AI to deliver transformative benefits without all the fearmongering and technobabble commonplace these days around AI discussions. As Schmarzo teaches us to think more like data scientists using street-tested tools and frameworks acquired through decades of data leadership, we come to see that AI is only as good (or bad) as we instruct it to be. With this knowledge, we become empowered citizens of this brave new world of AI and data science.

—Malcolm Hawker, Head of Data Strategy for Profisee Software

AI & Data Literacy: Empowering Citizens of Data Science is a great read that simplifies the complexity of the all-important topics and nuances of today's data and AI landscape into everyday language that everyday people can understand. As data and AI continue to evolve to play a bigger part in the lives of both businesses and everyday people, there's a huge chasm between the knowledge and understanding of the key topics and the reality of how it will change our world, creating fear and resistance. This book bridges that chasm head-on. A fascinating read for the data and technology community and an essential read for the business community.

—Kyle Winterbottom, CEO & Founder of Orbition Group

Bill continues his quest education on data, analytics, and AI – to make sure everyone understands what they are, what they can achieve, how they work, and how to deal with them. His new book, AI & Data Literacy: Empowering Citizens of Data Science, is not only for AI experts and practitioners but provides very didactic and pragmatic content to educate a broad audience of citizens while being very exhaustive and, as always, fun and easy to read. For all data and AI people, this is a highly recommended pick for your colleagues, friends, and family as education on the topic is obviously critical to face the upcoming changes in our society.

—Nicolas Averseng, Founder & CEO at YOOI

Bill's book comes at a critical time as people now realize that data and AI are part of everyone's job and part of the fabric of society. He explains in approachable and pragmatic ways why data literacy matters, how your data can be used for and against you, and the critical topic of AI ethics.

—Cindi Howson, Chief Data Strategy Officer at AI-Analytics ThoughtSpot, Host of the Award-Winning The Data Chief Podcast

Bill Schmarzo should get a Nobel prize or equivalent for his brilliant innovation in the data, analytics, and AI space. For the last 3 decades, Bill has innovated practically with his clients and produced a staggering amount of guidance, models, recipes, best practices, and thought leadership, and he shares it all freely. His lessons over the years are too many to mention and exceptionally relevant today. They have greatly matured the CDAO's arsenal of tools to be successful. His Business Benefit Analysis whitepaper in 1998 paved the way for how we prioritize initiatives today. Then there is the Big Data MBA Video Educational Series, and his two recent books, Thinking Like a Data Scientist and The Economics of Data, Analytics, and Digital Transformation. The CDAO community in the Middle East and Africa sees his approach as essential, and we appreciate the great relationship we have with Bill.

This book, AI & Data Literacy: Empowering Citizens of Data Science, will not only be essential in the offices of all CDAOs and their teams, but will be used by CEOs, board members, managers in the business units, front-line staff, and, well, everybody in business and technology. One of the most well-known sayings these days is "AI will not take over your job. Someone who uses AI will take over your job." Data literacy is still a very hot topic as businesspeople aspire to get business value from data. Bill has taken brilliant snippets of his repertoire of teachings and has again created a framework to empower us all to use data and AI responsibly and get the most value out of it. The AI and Data Literacy Educational Framework used throughout the book is once again a recipe that will be essential in corporate AI and data literacy programs.

—Debbie Botha, Women in AI Global Chief Partnership Officer, Dalebrook Media Middle East Managing Director

I really like the way this book puts people and the human experience deep at the center of AI, where others are desperately trying to automate everybody out. Bill is enabling everybody to have enough appreciation and knowledge to manage in the new world of ubiquitous AI, and that is how we move everybody forward.

—Jon Cooke, AI and Data Product Specialist

Contributor

About the author

Bill Schmarzo, the Dean of Big Data, is currently the Head of Customer Data Innovation at Dell Technologies. In his spare time, he is a lecturer at Iowa State University and Coe College (Cedar Rapids, IA), a University of San Francisco School of Management Executive Fellow, and an Honorary Professor at the School of Business and Economics at the National University of Ireland-Galway, where he teaches and mentors students in his course *Big Data MBA* and *Thinking Like a Data Scientist*. He is the author of four books: *Big Data: Understanding How Data Powers Big Business, Big Data MBA: Driving Business Strategies with Data Science, The Art of Thinking Like a Data Scientist*, and *The Economics of Data, Analytics, and Digital Transformation*. He has written over 300 blogs for Data Science Central, appeared on countless podcasts, has given numerous keynote presentations and university lectures, and is an active social media lightning rod on the topics of data science, artificial intelligence, data economics, design thinking, and team empowerment.

This book holds a special significance as it is the first book that I've written since moving back to Iowa in August 2022. Both my wife, Carolyn, and I were born in Iowa and met at Coe College in Cedar Rapids, IA. However, returning to Iowa after spending nearly three decades in Palo Alto and Silicon Valley did create a wee bit of apprehension. Nevertheless, I am immensely grateful to the numerous individuals who played a crucial role in supporting me throughout this transition period, enabling me to find new opportunities to flourish and grow.

First, my family members. I've already mentioned my wife, Carolyn, who endured my early mornings and restless nights wrestling with the book, and provided motivation (a.k.a. a swift kick in the butt) whenever I left like I'd reached the end of my rope. Thanks to my two sons and their wives who blessed us with our first grandchildren this past year – Alec and Dorian with granddaughter Emerson, and Max and Kelsey with grandson Campbell. Can't wait to start spoiling them (and helping them master that 3-point shot).

I'd also like to acknowledge my creative daughter, Amelia, who followed in her dad's footsteps to recently get her graduate degree from Emerson College in Digital Marketing and Data Analytics. Yes, we are a family that believes in the liberating power of AI and data literacy.

There were numerous friends who were instrumental in smoothing our transition back to Iowa, including Steve, David, Lori, Navin, Rod, Dave, Barb, Chantel, Kevin, Dawn, Brian, Jenny, Murugan, Armel, Peg, Dr. Buck, Rick, Marcia, Chuck, Amy, Ranjeetha, Russ, Kiran, Ted, Vrashank, Keri, Greg, Sudhir, Oliver, Daniel, Ant, Rob, Mike, Julie, Teresa, John, Bryan, Rob, Brenda, and Neal. I want to also thank my LinkedIn colleagues who are instrumental in providing me feedback and ideas whenever I engage on LinkedIn, including Samir, Somil, Mark, Jon, Christopher, Fred, Henrik, Dr. Anne-Marie, Dr. Mark, Debbie, Sharon, Malcolm, Jeff, Kyle, Benjamin, Kevin, Anders, J. Brian, Dan, Chris, Michael, Cindi, Mina, Vincent, Kurt, Assaf, Wayne, Randy, Tom, and so many more that I have missed but whose friendship I sincerely appreciate.

Special thanks to my Big Data MBA class lecturers, including John, John (again), Doug, Dan, Josh, Renee, and Brent. Also, thanks to my favorite Ingersoll Avenue Caribou Coffee crew (Alyssa, Fiona, Allison, Rachel, Emily, Kami, Jerzye, Hannah, Bailey, Nevean, Liv, Uat, Sophie, and Kelsey) for keeping my chai tea lattes hot. And, of course, to the absolutely best neighbors and friends with whom one could be blessed in Katie, Michael, Kennedy, Warren, and Allison (by the way, can I borrow your snow blower again?).

I want to express a huge appreciation for the Packt crew of Tanya D'cruz, Tushar Gupta, Aniket Shetty, and Janice Gonsalves, who were both patient and demanding in getting the most out of me in writing this book. If the book makes sense and the chapters flow smoothly, you can thank them for that!

I want to thank my students at Iowa State University and Coe College (all of whom must have watched Tom Hanks, in the movie Big, bravely raise his hand and feel empowered to say, "I don't get it.") and the clients with whom I have the good fortune to work. Every conversation leads to new learnings, and that's great for someone who doesn't have time for green bananas!

I also want to thank Dr. Wei Lin (my former Chief Data Scientist and the smartest, humblest person that I know) and Maria Parysz (CEO and Founder of three companies: Elephant AI, RecoAI, and LogicAI) for their assistance on my chapter on Generative AI and ChatGPT. Their guidance proved invaluable in simplifying this complex topic and its enabling technologies.

Finally, I want to express my sincere gratitude to Renee Lahti for her invaluable assistance in reviewing the flow and content of this book. Renee's exceptional skills as a Chief Data Officer, evident in her deep understanding of data science, data economics, and design thinking, make her the best CDO I've ever met. Her expertise shines through in every endeavor and team she leads. I feel incredibly fortunate that Renee took the time to review this book.

Join our book's Discord space

Join our Discord community to meet like-minded people and learn alongside more than 4000 people at:

https://packt.link/data

Table of Contents

Preface

Notice the cover of this book. Simple. Straightforward. No hyperbole about the extinction of humankind. No outrageous claims about massive human unemployment. Just a simple cover with a simple title to reflect the simple concept of **Artificial Intelligence** (**AI**).

Here is the simple truth about AI: AI will do exactly what you train it to do. Yes, AI can continuously learn and adapt with minimal human intervention, which scares people. However, the actions AI takes will be guided 100% by the user-defined outcomes and the measures against which outcome effectiveness will be measured. And all of these are 100% defined by you.

To design, develop, and manage AI effectively, adopting a holistic approach is paramount, and it calls for the active participation of everyone. The objective of this book is to simplify the discussion around AI and equip everyone with the knowledge to ensure AI is working for our benefit. By empowering everyone as Citizens of Data Science and fostering fundamental AI and data literacy, we can encourage active engagement that ensures AI's benefits are accessible to all.

I hope you enjoy reading and learning from the book as much as I did researching, testing, learning, relearning, and writing it. I hope you enjoy your AI and data literacy journey of becoming a Citizen of Data Science!

Who this book is for

This book is written for three segments of modern-day citizens:

- *Segment #1* comprises of individuals who seek a deeper understanding of AI and data, particularly regarding their impact on their everyday life. These individuals aspire to gain enough knowledge about AI and data to engage thoughtfully and respectfully with different perspectives and opinions, enabling them to independently evaluate the advantages and risks associated with AI and data.

- *Segment #2* encompasses individuals who are actively seeking to comprehend how AI and data can enhance both their personal lives and professional careers. With a focus on their careers, these individuals seek to understand future educational and personal development requirements. These folks are motivated to gain a better understanding of how AI and data applies directly to their lives, preparing them to grow and advance personally and professionally.

- *Segment #3* consists of individuals who are actively seeking to engage in the definition and oversight of rules and regulations governing the ethical, responsible, and meaningful design and deployment of AI. These individuals are driven by a desire to ensure that all voices and perspectives are considered, aiming to protect society from the careless and malevolent application of AI. Their goal is to create a safe and inclusive environment, where the potential risks and adverse impacts of AI are mitigated while maximizing its benefits for everyone.

While the book delves into some technical aspects, its goal is to explain these topics in a pragmatic manner. The book seeks to help everyone understand key technologies and concepts so they can participate in the discussions about the future applications and potential ramifications of these technologies and concepts. The book offers different ways of engaging with the content, so that anyone who wants to become a Citizen of Data Science can find a suitable and confident way of participating.

What this book covers

Chapter 1, Why AI and Data Literacy?, sets the groundwork for understanding why AI and data literacy is a conversation that must include everyone. The chapter highlights the rapid growth of AI in our everyday lives that impact society. The chapter also introduces the AI and Data Literacy Educational Framework that we will use throughout the book to guide our AI and data literacy education.

Chapter 2, Data and Privacy Awareness, ensures that everyone has a shared understanding of what we mean by the term big data and why it's more valuable (and dangerous) than regular data. We also outline new technology developments with the **Internet of Things (IoT)** and how your data is captured and used in real time to monitor and influence your decisions. Discussing some regulatory efforts to protect your data and preserve your privacy, we will also learn how organizations monetize personal data for their benefit.

Chapter 3, Analytics Literacy, is one of the more technical chapters in the book. But everyone must understand the different levels of analytics and how they can be used to uncover market, society, environmental and economic insights that can lead to better, more informed decisions. If data is the new oil, then analytics is the exploration, mining, extraction, and production tools we use to convert raw oil into products of value.

Chapter 4, Understanding How AI Works, like the title suggests, dives deep into AI and how it works. We will discuss the importance of ascertaining or determining user intent to frame your AI model development and provide a conceptual understanding of the AI utility function – the weighted portfolio of variables and metrics that the AI models will use to guide its relentless optimization efforts.

Chapter 5, Making Informed Decisions, explores the decision-making traps we fall into that lead to suboptimal, bad, and even dangerous choices. As a solution, we will introduce decision-making strategies, like the decision matrix, OODA, and so on, that everyone can and should use to leverage AI and data to make more informed decisions.

Chapter 6, Prediction and Statistics, provides a short primer on statistics, probabilities, predictions, and confidence levels. We will discuss how we can use statistics to help us improve the odds of making more effective and safer decisions in a world of constant economic, environmental, political, societal, and healthcare disruption.

Chapter 7, Value Engineering Competency, will explore how organizations of all sizes can leverage AI and data to engineer or create "value." We will present a framework for understanding how organizations define value and then identify the KPIs and use to measure their value creation effectiveness. We will also discuss why "economies of learning" are more powerful than "economies of scale" in a digital-centric world.

Chapter 8, Ethics of AI Adoption, describes some leading-edge ideas on how organizations and society can leverage economic concepts to transparently instrument and measure ethics and ensure that AI-based machines are working for humans rather than the other way around.

Chapter 9, Cultural Empowerment, will delve into the power and importance of empowerment to ensure that everyone has a voice in deciding and defining how best to leverage AI and data from a personal perspective. We will discuss how we must become "more human" to thrive alongside AI.

Chapter 10, ChatGPT Changes Everything, will provide a short primer on **Generative AI (GenAI)** products such as OpenAI ChatGPT, Microsoft Bing, and Google Bard. We will discuss how GenAI products work and the underlying technologies that make GenAI so effective in replicating human intelligence. Finally, we'll assess how one can apply the 6 components of the AI and Data Literacy Framework to use GenAI to deliver more relevant, meaningful, responsible, and ethical outcomes.

To get the most out of this book

What are the pre-requisites for this book? Simple – an open mind, an insatiable urge to learn, and the passion and fearlessness to get involved in the AI conversation. You must be willing and empowered in ensuring that your voice, and the voices of others, are being heard in this all-important AI conversation.

Download the color images

We also provide a PDF file that has color images of the screenshots/diagrams used in this book. You can download it here: `https://packt.link/rsXZb`.

Conventions used

There are a number of text conventions used throughout this book.

Bold: Indicates a new term, an important word, or words that you see on the screen . Words in menus or dialog boxes also appear in the text like this. For example: "Hit the **Finish Login** button at the bottom of the screen."

Warnings or important notes appear like this.

Tips and tricks appear like this.

Get in touch

Feedback from our readers is always welcome.

General feedback: Email feedback@packtpub.com, and mention the book's title in the subject of your message. If you have questions about any aspect of this book, please email us at questions@packtpub.com.

Errata: Although we have taken every care to ensure the accuracy of our content, mistakes do happen. If you have found a mistake in this book we would be grateful if you would report this to us. Please visit, http://www.packtpub.com/submit-errata, selecting your book, clicking on the Errata Submission Form link, and entering the details.

Piracy: If you come across any illegal copies of our works in any form on the Internet, we would be grateful if you would provide us with the location address or website name. Please contact us at copyright@packtpub.com with a link to the material.

If you are interested in becoming an author: If there is a topic that you have expertise in and you are interested in either writing or contributing to a book, please visit http://authors.packtpub.com.

Share your thoughts

Once you've read *AI & Data Literacy*, we'd love to hear your thoughts! Scan the QR code below to go straight to the Amazon review page for this book and share your feedback.

https://packt.link/r/1835083501

Your review is important to us and the tech community and will help us make sure we're delivering excellent quality content.

Download a free PDF copy of this book

Thanks for purchasing this book!

Do you like to read on the go but are unable to carry your print books everywhere? Is your eBook purchase not compatible with the device of your choice?

Don't worry, now with every Packt book you get a DRM-free PDF version of that book at no cost.

Read anywhere, any place, on any device. Search, copy, and paste code from your favorite technical books directly into your application.

The perks don't stop there, you can get exclusive access to discounts, newsletters, and great free content in your inbox daily

Follow these simple steps to get the benefits:

1. Scan the QR code or visit the link below

https://packt.link/free-ebook/9781835083505

2. Submit your proof of purchase
3. That's it! We'll send your free PDF and other benefits to your email directly

1

Why AI and Data Literacy?

Artificial Intelligence (**AI**) is quickly becoming infused into the very fabric of our everyday society. AI already influences decisions in employment, credit, financing, housing, healthcare, education, taxes, law enforcement, legal proceedings, travel, entertainment, digital marketing, social media, news dissemination, content distribution, pricing, and more. AI powers our GPS maps, recognizes our faces on our smartphones, enables robotic vacuums that clean our homes, powers autonomous vehicles and tractors, helps us find relevant information on the web, and makes recommendations on everything from movies, books, and songs to even who we should date!

And if that's not enough, welcome to the massive disruption caused by AI-powered chatbots like OpenAI's ChatGPT and Google's Bard. The power to apply AI capabilities to massive data sets, glean valuable insights buried in those massive data sets, and respond to user information requests with highly relevant, mostly accurate, human-like responses has caused fear, uncertainty, and doubt about people's futures like nothing we have experienced before. And remember, these AI-based tools only learn and get smarter the more that they are used.

Yes, ChatGPT has changed everything!

In response to this rapid proliferation of AI, **STEM** (**Science**, **Technology**, **Engineering**, and **Mathematics**) is being promoted across nearly every primary and secondary educational institution worldwide to prepare our students for the coming AI tsunami. Colleges and universities can't crank out data science and machine learning curriculums, classes, and graduates fast enough.

But AI and data literacy are more than just essential for the young. 72-year-old congressman Rep. Don Beyer (Democrat Congressman from Virginia) is pursuing a master's degree in machine learning while balancing his typical congressman workloads to be better prepared to consider the role and ramifications of AI as he writes and supports the legislation.

Thomas H. Davenport and DJ Patil declared in the October 2016 edition of The Harvard Business Review that data science is the sexiest job in the 21st century[1]. And then, in May 2017, The Economist anointed data as the world's most valuable resource[2].

"Data is the new oil" is the modern organization's battle cry because in the same way that oil drove economic growth in the 20th century, data will be the catalyst for economic growth in the 21st century.

But the consequences of the dense aggregation of personal data and the use of AI (neural networks and data mining, deep learning and machine learning, reinforcement learning and federated learning, and so on) could make our worst nightmares come true. Warnings are everywhere about the dangers of poorly constructed, inadequately defined AI models that could run amok over humankind.

> *"AI, by mastering certain competencies more rapidly and definitively than humans, could over time diminish human competence and the human condition itself as it turns it into data. Philosophically, intellectually — in every way — human society is unprepared for the rise of artificial intelligence."*
>
> *—Henry Kissinger, MIT Speech, February 28, 2019*

> *"The development of full artificial intelligence (AI) could spell the end of the human race. It would take off on its own and re-design itself at an ever-increasing rate. Humans, limited by slow biological evolution, couldn't compete and would be superseded."*
>
> *—Stephen Hawking, BBC Interview on December 2, 2014*

> *"Powerful AI systems should be developed only once we are confident that their effects will be positive and their risks will be manageable."*
>
> *—Future of Life Institute (whose membership includes Elon Musk and Steve Wozniak) on March 29, 2023*

There is much danger in the rampant and untethered growth of AI. However, there is also much good that can be achieved through the proper and ethical use of AI. We have a once-in-a-generation opportunity to leverage AI and the growing sources of big data to power unbiased and ethical actions that can improve everybody's quality of life through improved healthcare, education, environment, employment, housing, entertainment, transportation, manufacturing, retail, energy production, law enforcement, and judicial systems. This means that we need to educate everyone on AI and data literacy. That is, we must turn everyone into **Citizens of Data Science**.

AI and data literacy can't just be for the high priesthood of data scientists, data engineers, and ML engineers. We must prepare *everyone* to become Citizens of Data Science and to understand where and how AI can transform our personal and professional lives by reinventing industries, companies, and societal practices to fuel a higher quality of living for everyone.

In this first chapter, we'll discuss the following topics:

- History of literacy
- Understanding AI
- Data + AI: Weapons of math destruction
- Importance of AI and data literacy
- What is ethics?
- Addressing AI and data literacy challenges

History of literacy

Literacy is the ability, confidence, and willingness to engage with language to acquire, construct, and communicate meaning in all aspects of daily living. The role of literacy encompasses the ability to communicate effectively and comprehend written or printed materials. Literacy also includes critical thinking skills and the ability to comprehend complex information in various contexts.

Literacy programs have proven to be instrumental throughout history in elevating the living conditions for all humans, including:

- The development of the printing press in the 15th century by Johannes Gutenberg was a pivotal literacy inflection point. The printing press enabled the mass production of books, thereby making books accessible to all people instead of just the elite.
- The establishment of public libraries in the 19th century played a significant role in increasing literacy by providing low-cost access to books and other reading materials regardless of class.

- The introduction of compulsory education in the 19th and early 20th centuries ensured that more people had access to the education necessary to become literate.

- The advent of television and radio in the mid-20th century provided new methods to improve education and promote literacy to the masses.

- The introduction of computer technology and the internet in the late 20th century democratized access to the information necessary to learn new skills through online resources and interactive learning tools.

Literacy programs have provided a wide range of individual and societal benefits too, including:

- **Improved economic opportunities**: Literacy is a critical factor in economic development. It helps people acquire the skills and knowledge needed to participate in the workforce and pursue better-paying jobs.

- **Better health outcomes**: Literacy is linked to better health outcomes, as literate people can better understand health information and make informed decisions about their health and well-being.

- **Increased civic participation**: Literacy enables people to understand and participate in civic life, including voting, community engagement, and advocacy for their rights and interests.

- **Reduced poverty**: Literacy is critical in reducing poverty, as it helps people access better-paying jobs and improve their economic prospects.

- **Increased social mobility**: Literacy can be a critical factor in upward social mobility, as it provides people with the skills and knowledge needed to pursue education, job training, and other opportunities for personal and professional advancement.

We need to take the next step in literacy, explicitly focusing on AI and data literacy to support the ability and confidence to seek out, read, understand, and intelligently discuss and debate how AI and big data impact our lives and society.

Understanding AI

Okay, before we go any further, let's establish a standard definition of AI.

An AI model is a set of algorithms that seek to optimize decisions and actions by mapping probabilistic outcomes to a utility value within a constantly changing environment...with minimal human intervention.

Let's simplify the complexity and distill it into these key takeaways:

- Seeks to optimize its decisions and actions to achieve the desired outcomes as framed by user intent
- Interacts and engages within a constantly changing operational environment
- Evaluates input variables and metrics and their relative weights to assign a utility value to specific decisions and actions (AI utility function)
- Measures and quantifies the effectiveness of those decisions and actions (measuring the predicted result versus the actual result)
- Continuously learns and updates the weights and utility values in the AI utility function based on decision effectiveness feedback

...all of that with minimal human intervention.

We will dive deeper into AI and other advanced analytic algorithms in *Chapters 3* and *4*.

Dangers and risks of AI

The book *1984* by George Orwell, published in 1949, predicts a world of surveillance and citizen manipulation in society. In the book, the world's leaders use propaganda and revisionist history to influence how people think, believe, and act. The book explores the consequences of totalitarianism, mass surveillance, repressive regimentation, propagandistic news, and the constant redefinition of acceptable societal behaviors and norms.

The world described in the book was modeled after Nazi Germany and Joseph Goebbels' efforts to weaponize propaganda – the use of biased, misleading, and false information to promote a particular cause or point of view – to persuade everyday Germans to support a maniacal leader and his criminal and immoral view for the future of Germany.

But this isn't just yesteryear's challenge. In August 2021, Apple proposed to apply AI across the vast wealth of photos captured by their iPhones to detect child pornography[3].

Apple has a strong history of protecting user privacy. Twice, by the Justice Department in 2016 and the US Attorney General in 2019, Apple was asked to create a software patch that would break the iPhone's privacy protections. And both times, Apple refused based on their beliefs that such an action would undermine the user privacy and trust that they have cultivated.

So, given Apple's strong position on user privacy, Apple's proposal to stop child pornography utilizing their users' private data was surprising. Controlling child pornography is certainly a top social priority, but at what cost? The answer is not black and white.

Several user privacy questions arise, including:

- To what extent are individuals willing to sacrifice their personal privacy to combat this abhorrent behavior?

- To what extent do we have confidence in the organization (Apple, in this case) to limit the usage of this data solely for the purpose of combating child pornography?

- To what extent can we trust that the findings of the analysis will not fall into the hands of unethical players and be exploited for nefarious purposes?

- What are the social and individual consequences linked to the AI model's *false positives* (erroneously accusing an innocent person of child pornography) and *false negatives* (failing to identify individuals involved in child pornography)?

These types of questions, choices, and decisions impact everyone. And to be adequately prepared for these types of conversations, we must educate everyone on the basics of AI and data literacy.

AI Bill of Rights

The White House **Office of Science and Technology Policy (OSTP)** released a document called *Blueprint for an AI Bill of Rights*[4] on October 4, 2022, outlining five principles and related practices to help guide the design, use, and deployment of AI technologies to safeguard the rights of the American public in light of the increasing use and implementation of AI technologies.

To quote the preface of the extensive paper:

> *"Among the great challenges posed to democracy today is the use of technology, data, and automated systems in ways that threaten the rights of the American public. Too often, these tools are used to limit our opportunities and prevent our access to critical resources or services. These problems are well documented. In America and around the world, systems supposed to help with patient care have proven unsafe, ineffective, or biased. Algorithms used in hiring and credit decisions have been found to reflect and reproduce existing unwanted inequities or embed new harmful bias and discrimination. Unchecked social media data collection has been used to threaten people's opportunities, undermine their privacy, or pervasively track their activity—often without their knowledge or consent."*

The paper articulates your rights when interacting with systems or applications that use AI (*Figure 1.1*):

- You should be protected from unsafe or ineffective systems.

- You should not face discrimination by algorithms; systems should be used and designed equitably.

- You should be protected from abusive data practices via built-in protections and have agency over how data about you is used.

- You should know that an automated system is being used and understand how and why it contributes to outcomes that impact you.

 Safe and Effective Systems
You should be protected from unsafe or ineffective systems.

 Algorithmic Discrimination Protections
You should not face discrimination by algorithms and systems should be used and designed in an equitable way.

 Notice and Explanation
You should know an automated system is being used and understand how it contributes to outcomes that impact you.

 Data Privacy
You should be protected from abusive data practices and have agency over how data about you is used.

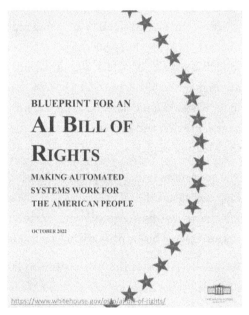

https://www.whitehouse.gov/ostp/ai-bill-of-rights/

Figure 1.1: AI Bill of Rights blueprint

The AI Bill of Rights is a good start in increasing awareness of the challenges associated with AI. But in and of itself, the AI Bill of Rights is insufficient because it does not provide a pragmatic set of actions to guide an organization's design, development, deployment, and management of their AI models. The next step should be to facilitate collaboration and adoption across representative business, education, social, and government organizations and agencies to identify the measures against which the AI Bill of Rights will be measured. This collaboration should also define the AI-related laws and regulations – with the appropriate incentives and penalties – to enforce adherence to this AI Bill of Rights.

Data + AI: Weapons of math destruction

In a world more and more driven by AI models, data scientists cannot effectively ascertain on their own the costs associated with the unintended consequences of false positives and false negatives. Mitigating unintended consequences requires collaboration across diverse stakeholders to identify the metrics against which the AI utility function will seek to optimize.

As was well covered in Cathy O'Neil's book *Weapons of Math Destruction,* the biases built into many AI models used to approve loans and mortgages, hire job applicants, and accept university admissions yield unintended consequences severely impacting individuals and society.

For example, AI has become a decisive decision-making component in the job applicant hiring process[5]. In 2018, about 67% of hiring managers and recruiters[6] used AI to pre-screen job applicants. By 2020, that percentage had increased to 88%[7]. Everyone must be concerned that AI models introduce bias, lack accountability and transparency, and aren't even guaranteed to be accurate in the hiring process. These AI-based hiring models may reject highly qualified candidates whose resumes and job experience don't match the background qualifications, behavioral characteristics, and operational assumptions of the employee performance data used to train the AI hiring models.

The good news is that this problem is solvable. The data science team can construct a feedback loop to measure the effectiveness of the AI model's predictions. That would include not only the false positives – hiring people who you thought would be successful but were not – but also false negatives – not hiring people who you thought would NOT be successful but, ultimately, they are.

We will deep dive into how data science teams can create a feedback loop to learn and adjust the AI model's effectiveness based on the AI model's false positives and false negatives in *Chapter 6*.

So far, we've presented a simplified explanation of what AI is and reviewed many of the challenges and risks associated with the design, development, deployment, and management of AI. We've discussed how the US government is trying to mandate the responsible and ethical deployment of AI through the introduction of the AI Bill of Rights. But AI usage is growing exponentially, and as citizens, we cannot rely on the government to stay abreast of these massive AI advancements. It's more critical than ever that, as citizens, we understand the role we must play in ensuring the responsible and ethical usage of AI. And that starts with AI and data literacy.

Importance of AI and data literacy

AI and data literacy refers to the holistic understanding of the data, analytic, and behavioral concepts that influence how we consume, process, and act based on how data and analytical assessments are presented to us.

Nothing seems to fuel the threats to humanity more than AI. There is a significant concern about what we already know about the challenges and risks associated with AI models. But there is an even bigger fear of the *unknown unknowns* and the potentially devasting unintended consequences of improperly defined and managed AI.

Hollywood loves to stoke our fears with stories of AI running amok over humanity (remember "Hello, Dave. You're looking well today." from the movie *2001: A Space Odyssey*?), fears that AI will evolve to become more powerful and more intelligent than humans, and humankind's dominance on this planet will cease.

Here's a fun smorgasbord of my favorite *AI-run-amok* movies that all portray a chilling view of our future with AI (and consistent with the concerns of Henry Kissinger and Stephen Hawking):

- *Eagle Eye*: An AI super brain (ARIIA) uses big data and IoT to nefariously influence humans' decisions and actions.
- *I, Robot*: Cool-looking autonomous robots continuously learn and evolve, empowered by a cloud-based AI overlord (VIKI).
- *The Terminator*: An autonomous human-killing machine stays true to its AI utility function in seeking out and killing a specific human target, no matter the unintended consequences.
- *Colossus: The Forbin Project*: An American AI supercomputer learns to collaborate with a Russian AI supercomputer to protect humans from killing themselves, much to the chagrin of humans who seem to be intent on killing themselves.
- *War Games*: The WOPR (War Operation Plan Response) AI system learns through game playing that the only smart nuclear war strategy is "not to play" (and that playing Tic-Tac-Toe is a damn boring game).
- *2001: A Space Odyssey*: The AI-powered HAL supercomputer optimizes its AI utility function to accomplish its prime directive, again, no matter the unintended consequences.

Yes, AI is a powerful tool, just like a hammer, saw, or backhoe (I guess Hollywood hasn't found a market for movies about evil backhoes running amok over the world). It is a tool that can be used for either good or evil. However, it is totally under our control whether we let AI run amok and fulfill Stephen Hawking's concern and wipe out humanity (think of *The Terminator*) or we learn to master AI and turn it into a valuable companion that can guide us in making informed decisions in an imperfect world (think of Yoda).

Maybe the biggest AI challenge is the *unknown unknowns*, those consequences or actions that we don't even think to consider when contemplating the potential unintended consequences of a poorly constructed, or intentionally nefarious, AI model. How do we avoid the potentially disastrous unintended consequences of the careless application of AI and poorly constructed laws and regulations associated with it? How do we ensure that AI isn't just for the *big shots* but is a tool that is accessible and beneficial to all humankind? How do we make sure that AI and the massive growth of big data are used to proactively *do good* (which is different from the passive *do no harm*)?

Well, that's on us. And that's the purpose of this book.

This book is about choosing... errr... umm... "good". And achieving *good* with AI starts with mastering fundamental AI and data literacy skills. However, the foundation for those fundamental AI and data literacy skills is ethics. How we design, develop, deploy, and manage AI models must be founded on the basis of delivering meaningful, responsible, and ethical outcomes. So, what does ethics entail? I've tried to answer that in the next section.

What is ethics?

Ethics is a set of moral principles governing a person's behavior or actions, the principles of *right and wrong* generally accepted by an individual or a social group. Or as my mom used to say, "Ethics is what you do when no one is watching."

Ethics refers to principles and values guiding our behavior in different contexts, such as personal relationships, work environments, and society. Ethics encompasses what society considers morally right and wrong and dictates that we act accordingly.

Concerning AI, ethics refers to the principles and values that guide the development, deployment, and management of AI-based products and services. As AI becomes more integrated into our daily lives, AI ethical considerations are becoming increasingly important to ensure that AI technologies are fair, transparent, and responsible.

We will dive deep into the topic of AI ethics in *Chapter 8*.

Addressing AI and data literacy challenges

What can one do to prepare themselves to survive and thrive in a world dominated by data and math models? Yes, the world will need more data scientists, data engineers, and ML engineers to design, construct, and manage AI models that will permeate society. But what about everyone else? We must train everyone to become Citizens of Data Science.

But what is data science? Data science seeks to identify and validate the variables and metrics that might be better predictors of performance to deliver more relevant, meaningful, and ethical outcomes.

To ensure that data science can adequately identify and validate those different variables and metrics that might be better predictors of performance, we need to ensure that we democratize the power of data science to leverage AI and big data in driving more relevant, meaningful, and ethical outcomes. We must ensure that AI and data don't create a societal divide where only the high priesthood of data scientists, data engineers, and ML engineers prosper. We must ensure that they don't benefit just those three-letter government agencies and the largest corporations.

We must prepare and empower everyone who is prepared to participate in and benefit from the business, operational, and societal benefits of AI. We must extend the AI Bill of Rights vision by championing a Citizens of Data Science mandate.

However, do you really understand your obligation to be a *Citizen* of Data Science? To quote my good friend John Morley on citizens and citizenship:

> *"Citizenship isn't something that is bestowed upon us by an external, benevolent force. Citizenship requires action. Citizenship requires stepping up. Citizenship requires individual and collective accountability – accountability to continuous awareness, learning, and adaptation. Citizenship is about having a proactive and meaningful stake in building a better world."*

Building on an understanding of the active participation requirements of citizenship, let's define the Citizens of Data Science mandate that will build our AI and data literacy journey:

Citizens of Data Science Mandate

Ensuring that everyone, of every age and every background, has access to the education necessary to flourish in an age where economic growth and personal development opportunities are driven by AI and data.

This Citizens of Data Science mandate would provide the training and pragmatic frameworks to ensure that AI and data's power and potential are accessible and available to everyone, and that the associated risks are understood so that we not only survive but thrive in a world dominated by AI and data.

The AI and Data Literacy Framework

To become a Citizen of Data Science, we need a set of guidelines – a framework – against which to guide our personal and organizational development with respect to understanding how to thrive in a world dominated by AI and data.

A *framework* is a structured approach that provides guidance, rules, principles, and concepts for solving a specific problem or accomplishing a particular task. Think of a framework as providing guard rails, versus railroad tracks, that proactively guide and benchmark our personal and professional development.

The **AI and Data Literacy Framework** provides those guard rails – and the associated guidance, rules, principles, and concepts – to ensure that everyone is aware of and educated on their role in ensuring the responsible and ethical definition, design, development, and management of AI models. It is a framework designed to be equally accessible and understandable by everyone.

We will use the AI and Data Literacy Framework shown in *Figure 1.2* throughout the book to help readers understand the different components of becoming Citizens of Data Science and ensure everyone has the skills and training to succeed in a world dominated by AI and data.

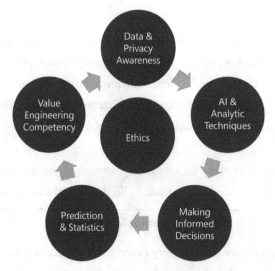

Figure 1.2: AI and Data Literacy Framework

This AI and Data Literacy Framework is comprised of six components:

1. **Data and privacy awareness** discusses how your data is captured and used to influence and manipulate your thoughts, beliefs, and subsequent decisions. This section also covers personal privacy and what governments and organizations worldwide do to protect your data from misuse and abuse.

2. **AI and analytic techniques** focuses on understanding the wide range of analytic algorithms available today and the problems they address. This chapter will explore the traditional, optimization-centric analytic algorithms and techniques so that our Citizens of Data Science understand what each does and when best to use which algorithms. And given the importance of AI, we will also have a separate chapter dedicated to learning-centric AI (*Chapter 4*). We will discuss how AI works, the importance of determining user intent, and the critical role of the AI utility function in enabling the AI model to continuously learn and adapt. This separate chapter dedicated to AI will also explore AI risks and challenges, including confirmation bias, unintended consequences, and AI model false positives and false negatives.

3. **Making informed decisions** or decision literacy explores how humans can leverage basic problem-solving skills to create simple models to avoid ingrained human decision-making traps and biases. We will provide examples of simple but effective decision models and tools to improve the odds of making more informed, less risky decisions in an imperfect world.

4. **Prediction and statistics** explains basic statistical concepts (probabilities, averages, variances, and confidence levels) that everyone should understand (if you watch sports, you should already be aware of many of these statistical concepts). We'll then examine how simple stats can create probabilities that lead to more informed, less risky decisions.

5. **Value engineering competency** provides a pragmatic framework for organizations leveraging their data with AI and advanced analytic techniques to create *value*. We will also provide tools to help identify and codify how organizations create value and the measures against which value creation effectiveness will be measured across a diverse group of stakeholders and constituents.

6. **AI ethics** is the foundation of the AI and Data Literacy Framework. This book will explore how we integrate ethics into our AI models to ensure the delivery of unbiased, responsible, and ethical outcomes. We will explore a design template for leveraging economics to codify ethics that can then be integrated into the AI utility function, which guides the performance of AI models.

This book will explore each subject area as we progress, with a bonus chapter at the end! But before we begin the journey, we have a little homework assignment.

Assessing your AI and data literacy

No book is worth its weight if it doesn't require its readers to participate.

Improving our AI and data literacy starts by understanding where we sit concerning the six components of our AI and data literacy educational framework. To facilitate that analysis, I've created the *AI and data literacy radar chart*. This chart can assess or benchmark your AI and data literacy and identify areas where you might need additional training.

A radar chart is a graphical method of capturing, displaying, and assessing multiple dimensions of information in a two-dimensional graph. A radar chart is simple in concept but very powerful in determining one's strengths and weaknesses in the context of a more extensive evaluation. We will use the following AI and data literacy radar chart to guide the discussions, materials, and lessons throughout the book:

Figure 1.3: AI and data literacy radar chart

This assignment can also be done as a group exercise. A manager or business executive could use this exercise to ascertain their group's AI and data literacy and use the results to identify future training and educational needs.

You will be asked to again complete the AI and data literacy radar chart at the end of the book to provide insights into areas of further personal exploration and learning.

In the following table are some guides to help you complete your AI and data literacy radar chart:

Category	Low	Medium	High
Data and privacy awareness	Just click and accept the website and mobile app's terms and conditions without reading	Attempt to determine the credibility of the site or app before accepting the terms and downloading	Read website and mobile app privacy terms and conditions and validate app and site credibility before engaging
Informed decision-making	Depend on their favorite TV channel, celebrities, or website to tell them what to think; prone to conspiracy theories	Research issues before making a decision, though still overweigh the opinions of people who "think like me"	Create a model that considers false positives and false negatives before making a decision; practice critical thinking
AI and analytic techniques	Believe that AI is something only applicable to large organizations and three-letter government agencies	Understand how AI is part of a spectrum of analytics, but not sure what each analytic technique can do	Understand how to collaborate to identify KPIs and metrics across a wide variety of value dimensions that comprise the AI utility function
Predictions and statistics	Don't seek to understand the probabilities of events happening; blind to unintended consequences of decisions	Do consider probabilities when making decisions but carry out a thorough assessment of the potential unintended consequences	Actively seek out information from credible sources to improve the odds of making an informed decision

Value engineering competency	Don't understand the dimensions of "value"	Understand the value dimensions but haven't identified the KPIs and metrics against which value creation effectiveness is measured	Understand the value dimensions and have identified the KPIs and metrics against which value creation effectiveness is measured
Ethics	Think ethics is something that only applies to "others"	Acknowledge the importance of ethics but are not sure how best to address it	Proactively contemplate different perspectives to ensure ethical decisions and actions

Table 1.1: AI and data literacy benchmarks

We are already using data to help us make more informed decisions!

Summary

In this chapter, we have seen that with the rise of AI and data, there is a need for AI and data literacy to understand and intelligently discuss the impact of AI and big data on society. The challenges and risks of AI include concerns about surveillance, manipulation, and unintended consequences, which highlight the importance of AI ethics and the need for responsible and ethical AI deployment.

This emphasizes the need to train individuals to become Citizens of Data Science in order to thrive in a data-driven world dominated by AI models. We proposed an AI and Data Literacy Framework consisting of six components, including data privacy, AI techniques, informed decision-making, statistics, value engineering, and AI ethics, to provide guidance and education for responsible and ethical engagement with AI and data.

We ended the chapter with a homework assignment to measure our current level of AI and data literacy. We will do the homework assignment again at the end of the book to measure just how much we learned along the journey, and where one might have to circle back to review selected subject areas.

Each of the next few chapters will cover a specific component of the AI and Data Literacy Framework. The exception is that we will divide the *AI and analytic techniques* component into two parts. *Chapter 3* will focus on a general overview of the different families of analytics and for what problems those analytics are generally used. Then, in *Chapter 4*, we will do a deep dive into AI – how AI works, the importance of the AI utility function, and how to construct responsible and ethical AI models.

Continuously learning and adapting...we're beginning to act like a well-constructed AI model!

References

1. Harvard Business Review. *Data Scientist: The Sexiest Job of the 21st Century* by Thomas Davenport and DJ Patel, October 2016: `https://hbr.org/2012/10/data-scientist-the-sexiest-job-of-the-21st-century`

2. The Economist. *The world's most valuable resource is no longer oil, but data*, May 2017: `https://www.economist.com/leaders/2017/05/06/the-worlds-most-valuable-resource-is-no-longer-oil-but-data?`

3. *Apple Plans to Have iPhones Detect Child Pornography, Fueling Privacy Debate*, Wall Street Journal, Aug. 5, 2021

4. Blueprint for an AI Bill of Rights: `https://www.whitehouse.gov/ostp/ai-bill-of-rights/`

5. *Vox. Artificial intelligence will help determine if you get your next job*: `https://www.vox.com/recode/2019/12/12/20993665/artificial-intelligence-ai-job-screen`

6. *LinkedIn 2018 Report Highlights Top Global Trends in Recruiting*: `https://news.linkedin.com/2018/1/global-recruiting-trends-2018`

7. *Employers Embrace Artificial Intelligence for HR*: `https://www.shrm.org/ResourcesAndTools/hr-topics/global-hr/Pages/Employers-Embrace-Artificial-Intelligence-for-HR.aspx`

Join our book's Discord space

Join our Discord community to meet like-minded people and learn alongside more than 4000 people at:

`https://packt.link/data`

2

Data and Privacy Awareness

Data is as common to our everyday lives as breathing and eating. Everything we say or do gets converted into data. **Data and privacy awareness** involves understanding how organizations capture, analyze, and use this personal data to influence your actions, behaviors, and beliefs.

If you have a smartphone, do anything on the web, use a credit card, or belong to a loyalty program, you already know that everything you do, post, or say is being tracked and captured. And that data is used by organizations to better understand our interests, passions, inclinations, and tendencies so they can better serve us, sell us more stuff, or influence how we think and act. Unfortunately, the odds are stacked in their favor in this relationship.

In this chapter, we will cover not only what data is being captured by organizations but also how these organizations use this data to persuade you. We will cover how the advent of big data transferred more power to the organizations that mastered the analysis of that data. We will also discuss some current data privacy initiatives.

In a nutshell, this chapter will discuss the following main topics:

- Understanding data and its types
- How is data collected?

- Understanding data privacy
- How organizations monetize your personal data

Your AI and data literacy starts by understanding what data is.

Understanding data

Data is a natural byproduct that records everything that is done, creating a comprehensive account of our activities and events. Data is individual facts, statistics, or pieces of information that are collected through observation or measurement. Data is also the facts and statistics collected to describe an entity (height, weight, age, location, origin, etc.).

Data can be either qualitative or quantitative: **qualitative** data describes something and **quantitative** data measures something. Within quantitative data, data can be either discrete or continuous. **Discrete** data can only take specific values (think whole numbers or predefined categories like age, gender, or zip code). **Continuous** data can represent any value (think fractions like 225.5 or 98.6). Data can be also be **factual** (weight and height) or **opinions** (favorite things and preferences). An example is shown in the following figure:

Data About Amelia's Dog Beau

Qualitative (observable) data:
- He is a dog
- He is black
- He has white hair on his chest
- He has short hair
- He can jump very high
- He is very fast
- He has lots of energy
- He likes to eat chicken
- His tug rag is Jake the Snake
- He hates fizzy water
- He thinks he can talk

Quantitative (measurable) data:

Discrete data:
- Male
- Four legs
- Two ears
- Two brothers

Continuous data:
- Weighs 56.2 lbs
- 22.5 inches tall
- 2.5 years old
- Jumps 26 inches

Figure 2.1: Data about Amelia's dog, Beau

Data is generated in every action we take – buying products, traveling to locations, watching television shows, calling someone, posting on social media, sending emails, manufacturing widgets, transporting boxes, repairing broken parts, filling our cars with gas, etc.

For example, a personal fitness device generates and captures data about your steps, the calories you burn, the number of stairs climbed, heart rate, the number of breaths you take per minute, rest time, sleep time, and more, as shown in the following figure:

Figure 2.2: Data recording my physical activities

Playing sports generates a flood of data recorded from every action and result during a game or match. In baseball, for example, we record balls and strikes, foul balls, singles, doubles, ground outs, double plays, runs scored, runs driven in, bases stolen, and much more, as shown in the following figure:

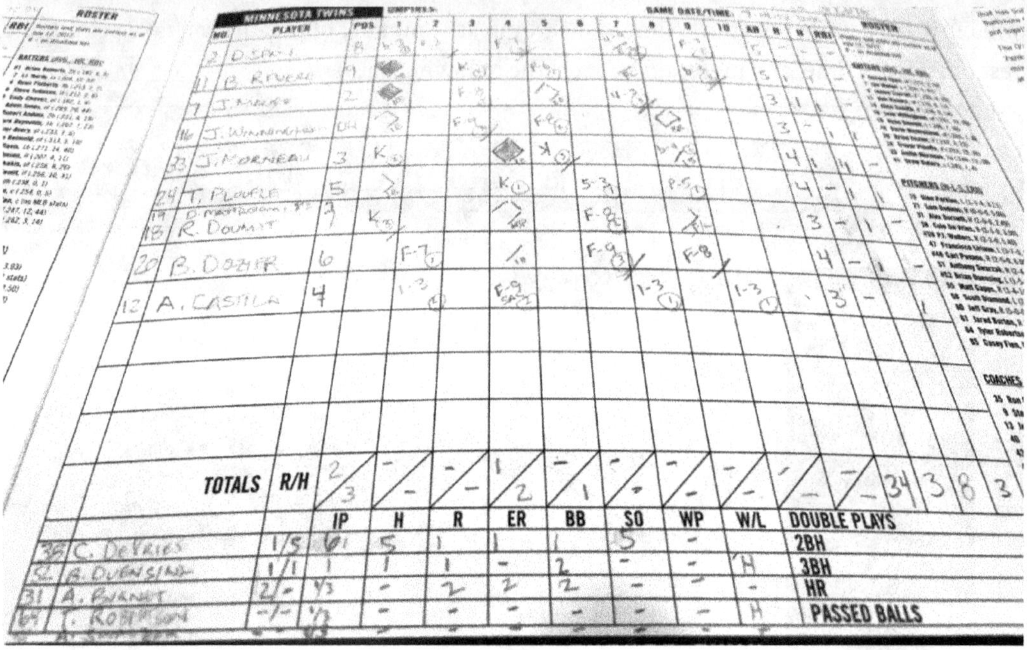

Figure 2.3: Data generated during a baseball game

You cannot avoid generating data as you live; every action you take is captured as data. For example, going to the grocery store generates data about your purchases captured by the retailer's **point-of-sales (POS)** system, as shown in the following receipt:

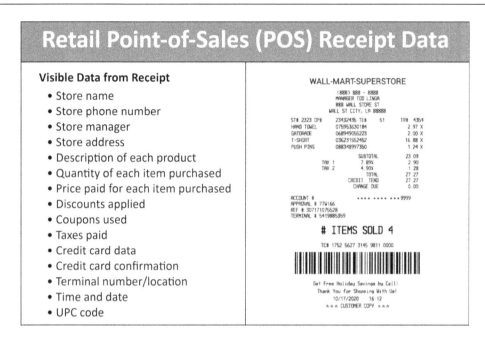

Figure 2.4: POS data generated from a grocery store visit

Data has always been a part of our everyday lives. But historically, most of that data was captured at an aggregated level and analyzed using averages. But using averages to make decisions, at best, yields average results. All of that changed with the advent of big data.

What is big data?

Data suddenly became interesting with the advent of big data.

Big data consists of massively large data sets of detailed transactions and engagements, which can be analyzed with advanced analytic algorithms and techniques to reveal patterns, trends, and relationships related to human or device behaviors and propensities.

The big data revolution had little to do with the size of data and everything to do with the granularity of the data. It wasn't the volume of data that powered leading organizations' value creation capabilities; it was the granularity of the data. Organizations could observe and capture an individual's detailed transactions, engagements, and activities for tens and hundreds of millions of customers. Yes, big data is Big Brother (a character from George Orwell's 1949 novel, *Nineteen Eighty-Four*).

Before big data, organizations only knew how many people watched a particular movie, how many people bought a specific product, how many people visited a particular theme park, or how many people ate at a specific restaurant. But with big data, organizations now know precisely what movies *you* watched and *your* reactions to each movie, what individual products *you* bought and with what other products, where *you* vacationed and *your* activities during your vacation, what restaurants *you* visited, and what *you* ordered and how *your* experience was.

Big data is about **YOU** and the capture and analysis of your transactions and engagements to determine your personal behavioral propensities and tendencies!

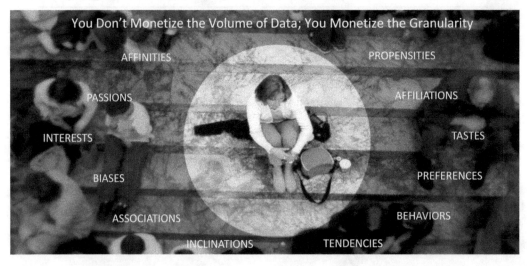

Figure 2.5: Big data is about YOU and your individual behaviors and propensities

Additionally, big data is just not numerical data. Big data includes social media photos and videos (think YouTube, Instagram, and TikTok), text messages, emails, log files, telephone conversations, meeting transcripts, surveillance videos, traffic camera videos, Google searches, chatbot conversations, and more than you can even imagine.

Here are just a few examples of where your personal big data is being collected and analyzed:

- Credit cards and digital payment apps track what you buy, what price you paid, where you bought the product or service, and the recency and frequency of those purchase behaviors.

- Loyalty cards link your personal demographic and sociodemographic data to your purchase history to provide insights into what products and services you are most likely to consume together and the recency and frequency of your shopping occurrences.

- Websites track what you read, when you read it, what ads you click, what ads you don't click, what keywords you search, etc.

- **Customer relationship management** (**CRM**) systems – including electronic health records – track every transaction, engagement, and conversation you have with anyone in that organization.

- Wi-Fi usage in coffee shops, airports, or hotel lobbies tracks the websites you access, the mobile apps you use, how much time you spend on those sites or apps, and your physical movement through a facility or building.

And if that's not enough, companies can combine additional data – much of it from third-party vendors – with the data captured at the time of customer engagement to provide further insights into your purchase and engagement behaviors, propensities, and tendencies.

Going back to our retail POS example, the retailer could generate additional, derived data by integrating the customer's purchase history, social media engagement, website visits, and customer loyalty card data as shown in the following figure:

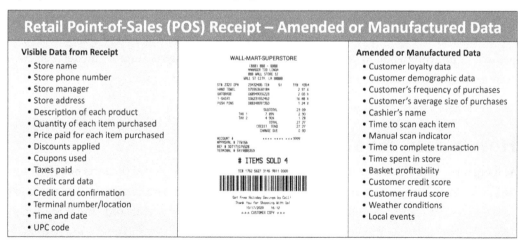

Figure 2.6 : Retailer amended and manufactured data

The combination of raw and derived data provides the foundation against which organizations apply advanced analytics to uncover your personal behavioral and performance propensities (an inclination or natural tendency to behave in a particular way), such as:

- Which products do you prefer? And which ones do you purchase together?
- When and where do you enjoy shopping?
- How often do you utilize coupons, and for which specific products?
- To what extent does price impact your purchasing habits?
- Which marketing campaigns and promotions do you typically respond to?
- Do the product combinations reflect your current phase of life
- Do you alter your purchase patterns in response to holidays and seasons?

There is nothing illegal about combining your consumer purchase data with other data sources to uncover and codify your preferences, patterns, trends, relationships, inclinations, and associations. The data these organizations collect is not within the boundaries of the law because you, as a consumer, have signed away (or "checked a box" away) your exclusive right to this engagement data.

What is synthetic data?

A relatively new development is the creation of synthetic data. Synthetic data is artificially generated data that is derived from actual data. Synthetic data can be used for training machine learning models when real-world data is not readily available or when privacy concerns prevent access to sensitive or private data. Synthetic data can also be used to enrich and increase the diversity of real data sets and address problems with AI model confirmation bias and ethical AI.

Additionally, synthetic data can be used for research and analysis when actual data is scarce, expensive, or difficult to obtain. Synthetic data can accelerate analysis, improve model predictive accuracy, and reduce costs in various business and operational use cases.

And then there's the Internet of Things…

How is data collected/captured?

As if organizations didn't capture enough data, organizations deployed the **Internet of Things** (**IoT**) to capture even more granular, low-latency customer and operational data. Add to the IoT data the ability to buy additional customer data from third-party aggregators, and these organizations were able to paint a very complete picture of their customers and how those customers interacted with their organizations.

Let's look at how these massive advancements impact data collection as a whole.

Sensors, surveillance, and IoT

IoT refers to the utilization of sensors, processing capabilities, software, and various technologies in physical objects. These objects are interconnected and share data with other devices and systems over the Internet or other communication networks.

Our smartphones send out a steady stream of data to the vendors of the smartphone apps regarding where you are, what you are doing, and what you might be saying. Connected vehicles constantly send data about your location, speeds, vehicle operations, and driving behaviors. Sports stadiums, theme parks, casinos, malls, stores, hospitals, airports, and other facilities leverage an army of video surveillance cameras to capture your movement and activities. Chatbots listen and record everything you say when seeking customer support, buying products, ordering food, and scheduling appointments.

Yes, IoT is expanding the presence of the organization by capturing, tracking, and analyzing customer engagement and operational activity at the *edges* of the organization; that is, at the organization's outmost and initial points of customer engagement and operational execution. The following data speaks for itself:

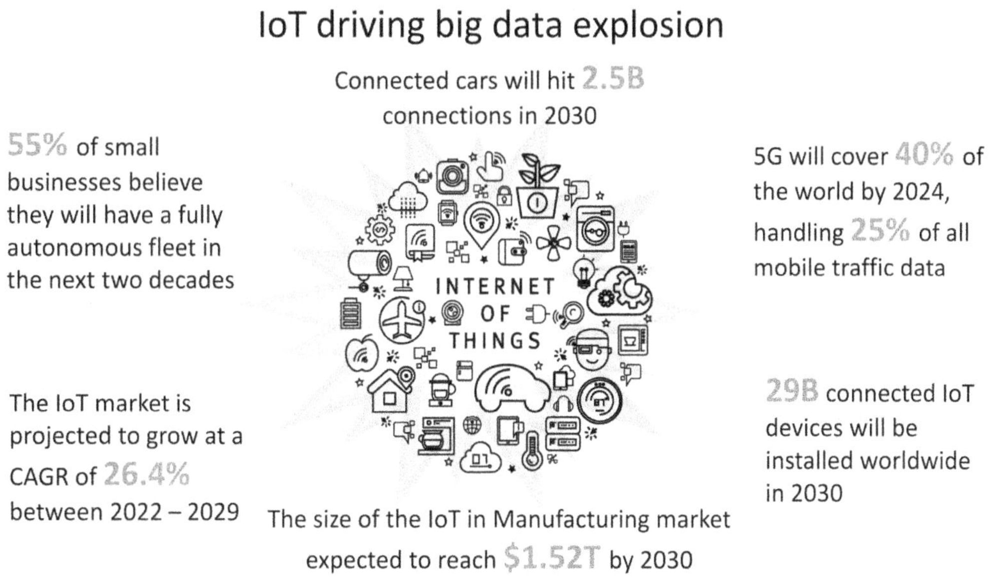

Figure 2.7: IOT creating an explosion of big data

The IoT edge refers to the IoT computing infrastructure that allows data processing and analysis to happen at the point where the data is generated. The business and operational value of the edge is realized through the **ingestion and analysis of and action on** that data as it is being created.

For example, let's say an autonomous vehicle is traveling down a highway at 70 miles per hour, and suddenly the car ahead blows a tire. There is no time for that observation to be sent to the cloud or a data center to be processed and analyzed and then for the appropriate action (stop or swerve) to be sent back down to the autonomous vehicle. In the time it takes for that process to occur, the autonomous vehicle will have t-boned the car ahead of it.

The edge enables new real-time business and operational use cases – everything from smart factories and smart cities to predictive maintenance, **robotic process automation (RPA)**, and location-based marketing – as depicted in the following image:

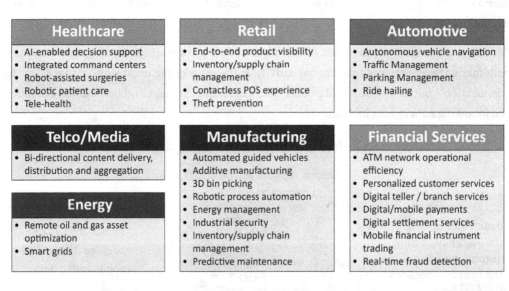

Figure 2.8: Edge-enabled use cases across industries

As we now understand the breadth of IoT's impact on our data, we all must be aware and vigilant of how IoT sensors, devices, and cameras capture data about us and how organizations will use that data for their business and operational purposes.

Third-party data aggregators

There are over 100 companies – such as Nielsen, Acxiom, Experian, Equifax, and CoreLogic – whose business model is built around acquiring, curating, analyzing, packaging, and selling your data. Unfortunately, many have no idea how much data these data aggregators are gathering about **YOU**!

Third-party data aggregators capture, aggregate, and sell nearly 3,000 behavioral attributes and calculated scores about your transactions, engagements, relationships, and interests, including:

- Socioeconomic status
- Economic stability
- Ethnicity
- Religion
- Health conditions such as:
    - Arthritis
    - Cardiac health
    - Diabetes
    - Disability
- Consumption of alcohol and tobacco
- Interest in gaming and gambling
- Social media engagement and relationships
- Home address
- Type of home
- Age of home
- The price paid for homes
- Taxes paid for homes
- Phone numbers
- Email addresses
- Life stage and lifestyle
- Family situation
- Banking accounts and insurance policies
- Properties owned
- Vehicles owned or leased
- Loans (mortgage, automobile, and line of credit)
- Income and net worth
- Credit card payment history
- Number of and ages of children

- Political views
- Newspaper and magazine subscriptions
- Favorite movie and television genre
- Favorite sports teams
- Club memberships
- Age
- Gender
- Education level
- Employment status

Yes, the level of information that these third-party data providers capture about you can be shocking. But let's be very clear – this is not illegal. You (sometimes unwittingly) agree to share your personal data when you sign up for credit cards, loyalty cards, and cell phone services and register for *free* services such as email, social media, Wi-Fi, newsletters, podcasts, webinars, mobile apps, and much more.

Companies combine this third-party data with their own data (captured through purchases, returns, marketing campaign responses, email correspondence, call center conversations, warranty cards, support sites, social media posts, etc.) to create an understanding of your interests, tendencies, preferences, inclinations, relationships, and associations so they can subsequently influence your purchases, actions, and beliefs.

Given the dire consequences of unauthorized access to our personal information by organizations, it is crucial to familiarize ourselves with the protective measures we have in place. Let's dive deeper and explore the various safeguards implemented to secure our data and find out whether or not these regulations are enough to protect our data privacy.

Understanding data privacy efforts and their efficacy

As discussed in the previous section, organizations, agencies, and third-party vendors are gathering and integrating data emitted from our daily activities. And they are using this treasure trove of data about us to influence our decisions, actions, and beliefs. Seems like the odds are stacked against the average citizen. However, government agencies around the world are trying to level the playing field and help to protect our data privacy.

Data protection and privacy laws

Governments worldwide are scrambling to avoid an avalanche of personal data privacy issues. Therefore, there are several regulatory efforts underway to try to protect your privacy, including:

- The **General Data Protection Regulation (GDPR)** was introduced in 2018 by the **European Union (EU)** on data protection and privacy in the EU and the European Economic Area. The GDPR is essential to EU privacy law and human rights law.

- The **California Consumer Privacy Act (CCPA)** of 2018 gives consumers more control over the personal information businesses collect about them, and the CCPA regulations guide the implementation of the law. The CCPA has become a model for other states like Colorado and Virginia looking to create their consumer privacy regulations.

- The **Personal Information Protection and Electronic Documents Act (PIPEDA)** is a Canadian privacy law governing private sector organizations' collection, use, and disclosure of personal information.

- The **Asia-Pacific Economic Cooperation (APEC) Privacy Framework** is a set of principles and practices for data protection developed by the APEC Forum.

Unfortunately, this patchwork effort to protect consumers' data privacy is insufficient. It dangerously trails the application of new technologies that enable unique and creative ways to capture more of your data, such as ChatGPT and Generative AI. Data privacy is an area where we should NOT wait for the government to protect us. Government policies and regulations will struggle to keep pace with the continuous technological and analytical advancements designed to capture more of our data! We must be prepared to safeguard ourselves.

Data privacy statements

A **data privacy statement** is a legal document that details how a website or mobile app can collect and use your personal data.

An organization's data privacy policy helps it comply with current data protection regulations. Unfortunately, a data privacy policy gives consumers a false sense of protection. Remember, corporate lawyers write these privacy policies to protect companies, not consumers. And that can be confirmed by the obscure and overly complex nature of how these privacy policies are written.

To quote the New York Times article *We Read 150 Privacy Policies. They Were an Incomprehensible Disaster*[1]:

> *Most privacy policies are verbose and full of legal jargon — and opaquely establish companies' justifications for collecting and selling your data. The data market has become the engine of the internet, and these privacy policies we agree to but don't fully understand help fuel it.*

To prove their point about privacy policies' obscure and overly complex nature, the New York Times generated a creative infographic that assesses the readability of 150 privacy policies. This infographic mapped each of the 150 privacy policies against the time it took an average person to read the policy and the level of complexity in the document from middle school to professional. Take a look at it here: `https://www.nytimes.com/interactive/2019/06/12/opinion/facebook-google-privacy-policies.html`. And you thought the book *Pride and Prejudice* was hard to read!

To make data privacy matters even more challenging, one needs to be aware of nefarious organizations operating around the edges of privacy laws and policies to capture even more of your data illegally. For example, iHandy Ltd. distributed the *Brightest Flashlight LED* Android app with over 10 million installations. Unfortunately for consumers who downloaded the app, iHandy Ltd. is headquartered in a country where consumer privacy laws are very lax compared to privacy laws in countries such as America, Europe, Australia, and Japan[2]. iHandy illegally mined the other apps on your Android phone and puled your privacy-protected personal data from those apps.

The Android *Brightest Flashlight LED* (with 10 million installations and created by iHandy Ltd.) collects the following data:

- Precise user location
- Access to users' contacts
- Access to send SMS messages
- Permission to directly call phone numbers
- Permission to reroute outgoing calls
- Access to the camera

- Access to record audio via the microphone
- Permission to read/write contents of USB storage
- Permission to read a phone's status and identity

But wait, there's more. With their always-on listening capabilities, a digital home assistant like Amazon Alexa or Google Assistant captures EVERYTHING being said in your home... all the time!

If you thought your in-home conversations were private, guess again! Even when there are privacy laws, law enforcement and government agencies can navigate around those privacy laws for probable cause. For example, in 2018, a New Hampshire judge ordered Amazon to turn over Amazon Echo recordings in a double murder case. Prosecutors hoped recordings captured by the couple's Amazon Echo could yield clues about who murdered two women in January 2017.

Surprising to the unsuspecting (or naïve), Amazon saves all recordings in its massive Amazon cloud. According to the search warrant, there was "probable cause" to believe that the Amazon Echo picked up "audio recordings capturing the attack" and "any events that preceded or succeeded the attack".[3] As a result, the data that someone didn't even know was being captured in their home was turned over to law enforcement.

Yes, the world envisioned by the movie *Eagle Eye*, with its nefarious, always-listening, AI-powered ARIIA is more real than one might think. Remember, digital media (and the cloud) has a long memory. Once you post or say something, expect it to be in the digital ecosystem *forever*.

How organizations monetize your personal data

We mentioned in the previous chapter that "data is the new oil". In the same way that oil drove economic growth in the 20th century, data will be the fuel that drives economic growth in the 21st century.

Companies collect and analyze your personal data with the objective of influencing your perspectives, decisions, and actions. Companies such as Facebook, Google, Amazon, Netflix, and Spotify monetize your data by uncovering the individual propensities and tendencies buried in your data and then using those personal propensities and tendencies to influence your purchase and usage decisions... and sometimes even your opinions.

Figure 2.9 shows how Google leverages your *free* search requests to create a market for advertisers willing to pay to place their products and messages at the top of your search results.

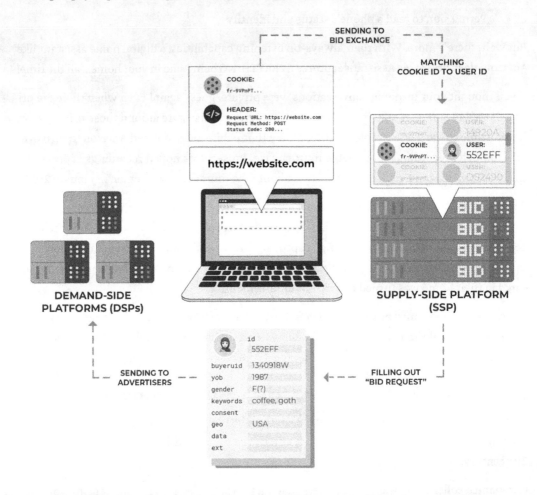

Figure 2.9: Data flows in a typical real-time bidding system (taken from eff.org/deep-links/2020/03/google-says-it-doesnt-sell-your-data-heres-how-company-shares-monetizes-and)

Here are other ways that Google *monetizes* your data:

- **Google Ads**: Google leverages AI to improve online product and service targeting based on a profile of your areas of interest.
- **Gmail**: Google integrates AI into its Gmail services to enhance customer experience such as *Intelligent Reply*, which enables Gmail to analyze the entire email and propose a relevant reply.

- **Google Assistant**: Google's voice assistant learns your areas of interest to make product and service recommendations based on your interests.

- **Google Maps**: One of my favorite Google products, Google uses AI to recommend a faster path to your desired destination. It even offers recommendations – such as nearby restaurants, gas stations, coffee shops, etc. – based on your interests.

- **Google Photos**: Google analyzes your photos using AI and suggests images and videos that you might want to share with friends and families.

Yes, your personal data helped Google achieve $189 billion in digital media revenue in 2021. Not a bad financial return for *free* customer service. But not all of this is bad.

Many of the highly personalized services and highly relevant recommendations that you receive are courtesy of organizations' excellent data acquisition, data management, and data science skills, which lead to improved consumer experiences, such as recommending the most efficient route home, products that are on sale that you might want, movies and songs that you might enjoy, and even potential *partners* with whom you might be able to share a life experience.

Many of these organizations provide you with something of *value* in return for your data, such as free email, social media platforms, personalized web experiences, free online games, free navigational services, and product and service discounts (in the case of loyalty programs). ChatGPT is another example of a free service that provides something of *value*. For example, ChatGPT can significantly accelerate your research, and in return, ChatGPT continually expands its knowledge based on human interaction and feedback to ensure the relevance and accuracy of its responses.

The key is that users need to be aware that there is a *price* for these *free* services, even if the price isn't as apparent as a monthly subscription fee.

Summary

In this chapter, we explored the differences between data and big data, and how organizations use your personal data to understand your tendencies and propensities. We discussed how technologies such as the IoT and third-party data aggregators capture and analyze your transactions and activities to learn even more about your personal tendencies and propensities. We then explored data privacy efforts, both at the federal and state government levels to protect your data privacy, and how some organizations can just decide to ignore those protections for their own nefarious means. We wrapped up the chapter with a look at how one leading data monetization company – Google – provides free services in exchange for your data, which they subsequently monetize in a number of perfectly legal ways.

So, how can one protect themselves from being abused by their own data? The first step is awareness and vigilance. We must always be aware of how organizations capture and exploit our data for their own purposes. We must always be vigilant about what data we share via the apps on our phones, the customer loyalty programs to which we belong, and our posts on websites and social media. But even then, disreputable organizations will skirt the data privacy laws to capture more of your data from their nefarious acts (spam, phishing, identity theft, ransomware, and more).

Lastly, countries have historically gone to war over possessing and controlling precious economic assets like oil. And we are already starting to see countries fighting digital wars to steal each other's data. Is it only a matter of time before these data wars, breaches, and attacks lead to armed conflict? These are issues we must be prepared to address as a society.

In the next chapter, we will get a wee bit technical and explore the broad realm of analytics, starting with Business Intelligence and progressing through supervised and unsupervised machine learning, deep learning, and eventually reinforcement learning. We will save the discussion and exploration of artificial intelligence for its own chapter… it deserves it!

References

1. New York Times. *We Read 150 Privacy Policies. They Were an Incomprehensible Disaster*: `https://www.nytimes.com/interactive/2019/06/12/opinion/facebook-google-privacy-policies.html`

2. Mobile Privacy. *What Do Your Apps Know About You?*: `https://symantec-enterprise-blogs.security.com/blogs/threat-intelligence/mobile-privacy-apps`

3. TechCrunch. *Judge orders Amazon to turn over Echo recordings in double murder case*: `https://techcrunch.com/2018/11/14/amazon-echo-recordings-judge-murder-case/`

Join our book's Discord space

Join our Discord community to meet like-minded people and learn alongside more than 4000 people at:

`https://packt.link/data`

3

Analytics Literacy

Before you read this chapter, just some advice – you may never be asked to program a neural network or an unsupervised machine learning algorithm, but it is essential that you have a rough idea of how these algorithms work and what these algorithms are good at doing. The goal of these next few pages is to demystify data science and these different algorithms so that everyone of every age is prepared to have an everyday analytics conversation.

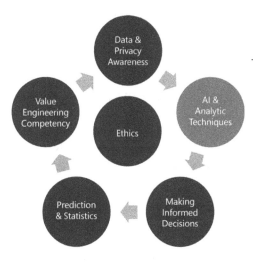

AI and analytics literacy is understanding how advanced analytic algorithms and concepts work – including machine learning, reinforcement learning, and deep learning – and what types of problems these analytical algorithms can be applied to.

This is the most challenging chapter of the book as it will provide a broad overview of the different types of advanced analytic algorithms and concepts. Think of this as a family of additional analytical capabilities versus a single tool. Then, in the next chapter, I will do a deep dive into AI.

 Be sure to check out the *Glossary* for definitions of some of the terms used in this chapter, such as data model, schema on load, and schema on read.

But before I explain the different categories of advanced analytics, we will first review the differences between **business intelligence (BI)** and data science. This is especially important given the predominance of BI as the bedrock of analytics for many organizations.

In a nutshell, this chapter will discuss the following topics:

- The differences between BI and data science
- The data science development process
- The analytics maturity index and how to navigate it

BI vs. data science

BI has been the foundation of organizations' analytic efforts for decades. Organizations have invested significant money and time into building, managing, and updating their BI environments and training and supporting business users in the use of BI tools. While BI was critical in monitoring business performance and reporting, it never provided the capabilities or frameworks to predict what was likely to happen and make prescriptive recommendations. Those were the capabilities that data science brought to the analytics effort.

Do not think of data science as a replacement for BI, however. Data science builds upon and extends organizations' capabilities to get value from their data but requires an entirely new analytics mindset.

What is BI?

BI interprets historical data to understand changes in a business better. BI has formed the foundation of organizations' analytics for decades.

BI is focused on generating reports, charts, and dashboards that tell the business and operational users what's happening to the business. Think of it as a report card upon which we can grade business and operational performance. Nearly every organization has BI capabilities that are readily available via spreadsheet tools such as Microsoft Excel, Google Sheets, or more advanced BI tools like Microsoft Power BI, ThoughtSpot, or Salesforce Tableau.

BI is software that provides a historical or retrospective view of a business. It interprets historical data to understand business and operational changes better. BI software typically analyzes structured operational data (numerical data stored in tables of rows and columns). It generates user-friendly views of the data through reports, dashboards, charts, and graphs supporting management's business assessments.

BI enables business analysts to interactively *slice and dice* the data to identify performance anomalies, create market share calculations, trend operational performance, and compare current performance with different time periods (the current performance versus last week's, last month's, last quarter's, or last year's).

For example, a BI analyst might create a report and dashboard that monitors product sales performance that integrates the product sales pipeline (from the sales management system) with product orders (from the order entry system), with product shipments (from the shipments system), with payments (from the accounts receivable system), and with returns (from the returns management system). This report and dashboard might compare the current period's sales performance to previous periods' sales performance (a week ago, a month ago, a quarter ago, or a year ago) to flag any areas of over- or under-performance. This data might be dumped into an **online analytic processing (OLAP)** cube so that business analysts can *drill into* the data to better understand the areas of under- and over-performance.

What is data science?

Data science is about identifying those variables and metrics that might be better predictors of performance.

Data science leverages much of the same historical data to provide predictions about what is likely to happen and then create recommendations based on those predictions on what actions to take next. In the past 15 years, data science has emerged to enable advanced analytics that predict what's likely to happen and prescribe recommendations as to what actions should be taken, given that prediction.

Data science introduced a completely new set of advanced analytic capabilities, such as supervised and unsupervised machine learning, deep learning/neural networks, reinforcement learning, and federated learning. And even today, the advancements in data science continue to evolve with new technologies such as the GenAI that enables OpenAI ChatGPT, Google Bard, and Microsoft Bing.

The rest of this chapter will talk extensively about data science and the advanced analytic tools that data science teams use to derive and drive new sources of customer, product, service, and operational value.

The differences between BI and data science

The most significant difference is that data science works with individual transactions. In contrast, BI works with aggregated data (it's hard to create a practical report or dashboard that reports and monitors the individual purchase behaviors of millions of customers).

The following figure highlights the complementary analytics value chain, from descriptive questions (supported by BI) to predictive analytics and prescriptive actions (supported by data science):

Analytics Value Chain: From Descriptive to Prescriptive

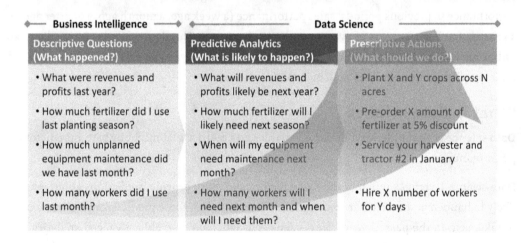

Business Intelligence		Data Science	
Descriptive Questions (What happened?)	**Predictive Analytics (What is likely to happen?)**	**Prescriptive Actions (What should we do?)**
• What were revenues and profits last year?	• What will revenues and profits likely be next year?	• Plant X and Y crops across N acres
• How much fertilizer did I use last planting season?	• How much fertilizer will I likely need next season?	• Pre-order X amount of fertilizer at 5% discount
• How much unplanned equipment maintenance did we have last month?	• When will my equipment need maintenance next month?	• Service your harvester and tractor #2 in January
• How many workers did I use last month?	• How many workers will I need next month and when will I need them?	• Hire X number of workers for Y days

Figure 3.1: Analytics Value Chain

Another way to view the differences between BI and data science can be seen in the following figure, which frames the BI and data science positioning from a business value (high to low) and timeframe perspective (analyzing past results versus predicting future results):

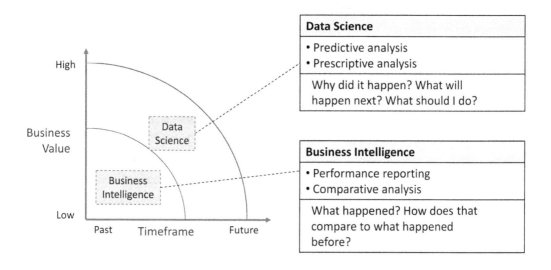

Figure 3.2: Differences between BI and data science

Another way to look at the differences and similarities between BI and data science is the nature of the role of a business analyst versus a data scientist, which is illustrated in the following figure:

Area	BI Analyst	Data Scientist
Focus	Reports, KPIs, trends	Patterns, correlations, models
Process	Static, comparative	Exploratory, experimental, visual
Data sources	Pre-planned, added slowly	On-the-fly, as needed
Transform	Upfront, carefully planned	In-database, on-demand, enrichment
Data quality	Single version of truth	Good-enough probabilities
Data model	Schema on load	Schema on query
Analytics	Retrospective, descriptive	Predictive, prescriptive, preventative

Figure 3.3: Comparison of business analyst and data scientist roles

While the preceding highlights some of the differences between BI and data science, the most significant difference is the highly structured BI development process (where the criterion for success is typically **defined** before the reports or dashboards are generated) versus the highly iterative, highly exploratory, failure-embracing data science development process (where the criterion for success is **discovered** as the predictive and prescriptive models are developed).

As I mentioned before, one of the challenges in appreciating data science is understanding the process or methodology that data science teams use to build their predictive and prescriptive analytic models. It's very different from traditional software development in the highly non-linear, recursive way that the analytic models are developed, validated, and operationalized.

Maybe the biggest difference between data science and traditional software development is that in software development, we define the criteria for success. In data science, we discover the criteria for success. Let's discuss that next!

Understanding the data science development process

Data science uses a highly iterative, collaborative development process to identify those variables and metrics that might be accurate predictors of performance. The data science development process supports testing, experimenting, failing, learning, unlearning, and retrying using a combination of advanced analytic algorithms, data transformation, and data enrichment techniques necessary to *discover* those variables and metrics.

The data science development process is a non-linear framework of rapid exploration, discovery, learning, testing, failing, and learning again. It drives collaboration between data scientists and data engineers and business and operational subject-matter experts and domain experts to ideate, explore, and test those variables and metrics that *might* be better predictors of performance.

Figure 3.4 highlights this highly non-linear, recursive approach that a data science team will use to build, test, learn, refine, and validate their predictive and prescriptive analytics models. This approach is based upon failure as a source of learning; you must push the edges of the data science process by exploring new techniques, new features, new data transformations, and different combinations of algorithms to build models that are better predictors of behaviors and performance.

If you ain't failin', you ain't learnin'.

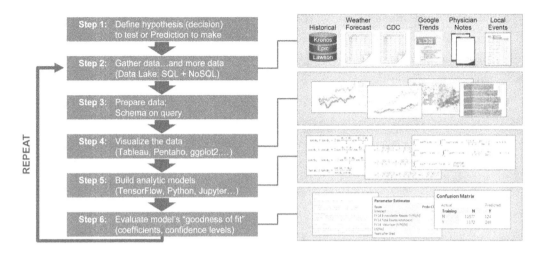

Figure 3.4: Data science collaborative development process

Let's look at the steps involved in the data science collaborative development process in more detail:

1. **Define the hypothesis that you are trying to address**: This step requires close collaboration between the business subject-matter experts (who understand the operational objectives, desired outcomes, key decisions, and the KPIs and metrics against which we will measure outcomes and decision effectiveness) and the data science team (who is responsible for massaging the data and building the analytic models that deliver the desired outcomes and improved decisions). We go into significant detail on this all-important step in *Chapter 7*.

2. **Gather data**: Based upon the problem that you are trying to solve and the decisions you are trying to improve, start gathering and exploring a wide variety of data sources in search of the variables and metrics that might be good predictors of behaviors and performance.

3. **Prepare data**: This is the heavy data engineering and data munging work to prepare the data for analytic modeling, including the cleansing, parsing, transformation, enrichment, sampling, aggregation, and integration of the data. This is the work necessary to ensure that the data is ready for the data scientist and their model exploration and development process.

4. **Visualize the data**: The data science team will create visualizations to help them better understand the content of the data with which they are working. These data visualizations include box-and-whisker charts, line charts, area charts, histograms, scatter plots, heatmaps, geolocation maps, and network graphs.

5. **Build analytic models**: This is where the rubber meets the road. The data scientists start exploring different data transformations, data enrichments, and combinations of analytic algorithms in search of the right orchestration of analytics and transformations that deliver the *best* results.

6. **Evaluate model's "Goodness of Fit"**: The data science team examines the results of their analytic model to ascertain the *Goodness of Fit* with respect to coefficients of correlation and confidence levels. The model's *Goodness of Fit* is measured and judged against the context of the costs of the model's false positives and false negatives. That is, are the model results "good enough" given the costs of the model being wrong?

Note that the analytic model's *Goodness of Fit* will be judged against these measures:

- **Precision** measures the correctness of positive predictions. It measures how accurately a model identifies positive instances out of all the instances it predicts as positive. It focuses on the correctness of the model's positive predictions.

- **Recall**, also known as sensitivity or the true positive rate, measures the ability to find all positive instances. This measure focuses on the model's ability to find all the positive instances, regardless of how many false positives it predicts.

- **Accuracy** measures overall model performance. It calculates the percentage of correct predictions (both true positives and true negatives) out of the total number of predictions.

If the results of the models are not good enough (which they typically are not), then the feedback from the process is fed back into *step 2* and the process starts over again… and again… and again…

Might is the crucial catalyst in the data science development process. The process will explore, test, and learn to identify those variables and metrics that *might* be better predictors of performance, but data science explorations will only yield teachings about what did not work. However, if you don't have enough *might* moments in your data science process, you'll never have any breakthrough moments. Or, to quote Thomas Edison about inventing the electric light bulb: "I have not failed. I've just found 10,000 ways that won't work."

The data science development process will test many combinations of data elements, data enrichment techniques, and a variety of analytic algorithms in an attempt to discover those variables and metrics that *are* better predictors of performance.

It is important to reiterate here that, this highly interactive process is not linear, which means that the process of building a model that is *good enough*, does not happen predictively. There will be many, many failures as the data science team explores different combinations of data sources, data transformations, and analytic algorithms in search of the results that are *good enough* given the costs of being wrong.

Note that most software development teams hate the highly unpredictable nature of the data science development process. But remember this: the software development process defines the criteria for success; the data science team discovers it.

The critical role of design thinking

One discipline that can dramatically improve the data science team's ability to deliver relevant, meaningful results is design thinking. Integrating design thinking concepts into the data science development process is critical in creating a mindset and culture of exploration, trying, failing, and learning between the data science team and business subject-matter experts.

Design thinking is a highly collaborative, iterative process that seeks to uncover and validate customer needs and desired outcomes via collaborative customer engagement within the context and constraints of the specific customer *journey*. Throughout the data science development process, design thinking drives ideation, exploration, and experimentation in tight collaboration with the business stakeholders, with an "all ideas are worthy of consideration" mindset.

Yes, design thinking is the secret sauce to creating an effective and empowering data science development process, as illustrated in the following figure:

Design Thinking Empowers Data Science

Design thinking involves observation to discover unmet needs within the context and constraints of a particular situation. It frames the opportunity and scope of innovation, generating creative ideas and testing and refining solutions. It creates a repeatable and scalable process for innovation.

Design Thinking

Design products this way...

Refine, tune, and predict this way...

Data Science

Data Science is a method of data analysis that automates analytical model building. Using algorithms that iteratively learn from data, *machine learning* allows computers to find hidden insights without being explicitly programmed where to look.

Learn about the audience for whom you are designing. *Who is my user? What matters to this person? What are their needs?*

Create a POV based on user needs and insights.

Brainstorm as many creative solutions as possible. *Wild ideas encouraged!*

Model one or more of your ideas to show to others. *How can I show my idea? Remember: a prototype is just a rough draft.*

Share prototype for feedback. *What worked? What didn't?*

Empathize

Ideate

Define

Prototype

Test

Analyze

Ideate

Tuning

Synthesize

Validate

Break down needs into base parts (decisions)

Combine separate elements in order to create a new "whole"

Brainstorm to process the product requirement into:
-Feature maps
-Classes
-Metrics
-Adaptive needs

Tune the model to boost accuracy. Avoid "over-fitting"

Meet inference performance metrics. Avoid "over-fitting"

Human Learning-Centered

Machine Learning-Centered

Figure 3.5: Design thinking empowers data science

To better understand the integration of design thinking with Data Science, let's examine the following table:

Design Thinking	Design Thinking + Data Science Synergies	Data Science
Empathize	Understand your target users and their base needs, such as objectives, decision-making criteria, desired outcomes, and measures of success.	Analyze
Define	Create a comprehensive understanding of users by identifying and analyzing their needs, key decisions, pains, and gains along their journey.	Synthesize
Ideate	Brainstorm as many creative solutions as possible based on users' desired outcomes and measures of success.	Ideate
Prototype	Model, critique, learn, tune, and model again to tune the model to boost the users' outcomes' relevance and accuracy.	Tuning

Test	Share a prototype with target users to gather, validate, value, and prioritize their feedback on the effectiveness vis-a-vis their desired outcomes and measures of success.	Validate

Table 3.1: Data science and design thinking combined

Now that we have a feel for how analytic models are built and the role that design thinking can play in the process, we want to understand the spectrum of different analytic algorithms and techniques that a data science team might use to build their predictive and prescriptive analytic models.

Navigating the analytics maturity index

 I struggled with this section, but not because explaining the different analytic algorithms and concepts was hard. For me, the complicated problem was how to classify and group these different algorithms in a way that makes it easier for the average Citizen of Data Science to understand where and how to apply these algorithms.

Leading organizations are cultivating a culture of continuous exploration, learning, adaptation, and re-learning. This iterative process involves gathering insights from every customer engagement to understand their preferences and behaviors better. Similarly, interactions with products enable organizations to gain knowledge about product performance and behaviors while engagement with employees, suppliers, and partners provides valuable opportunities to improve the effectiveness and efficiency of business operations. To create a continuous learning culture, organizations need to understand the **Analytics Maturity Index** – from reporting and predicting, to prescribing and autonomous analytics.

This Analytics Maturity Index helps organizations transition through the four levels of analytics maturity, through operational reporting (reporting on the status of the business and operations), predictive analytics (to predict what is likely to happen next), prescriptive analytics (to recommend a corrective or opportunistic action), and autonomous operations (self-learning and self-adapting with minimal human intervention).

Let's now dive into each of the four levels of analytics maturity.

Level 1: Operational reporting

Level 1 reports on historical performance and leverages comparison and benchmarking techniques to flag areas of under- and over-performance.

Level-1 analytics monitors the state of the business. Think of it as a report on the state of the business or operations. It leverages historical operational data to monitor the condition of the business through management reports and operational dashboards. Level-1 analytics compares the current performance to previous periods' performance to flag anomalies and generates management and operational alerts.

While several analytic capabilities fall into this classification, the most significant are BI and Six Sigma. We covered BI earlier in this chapter, so let's discuss Six Sigma.

Six Sigma is a set of management techniques intended to improve business processes by reducing the probability of an error or defect. Six Sigma is a process that uses statistics and data analysis to analyze operational data to improve cycle times while reducing defects to no more than 3.4 defects per million units or events. Six Sigma is used in many industries where there is a need to improve quality, reduce defects and variability, and optimize processes, including manufacturing, healthcare, finance, services, and technology.

For example, Six Sigma could be employed in manufacturing to flag production variances that could indicate future product quality problems and return issues later in the value chain. Six Sigma could also be used in healthcare to flag patient care deviations across care units that could indicate patient readmission or hospital-acquired infection problems.

Common Six Sigma tools include:

- **Value stream mapping** to illustrate and optimize the flow of materials and information within a production process.
- **Pareto charts** provide an informative visual highlighting the differences between different production data groups. This allows teams employing Six Sigma techniques to quickly and visually identify the most significant threats or risks to a production process.
- **Regression analysis** is a statistical approach to quantifying the negative or positive relationships among multiple variables in a production process. That is, one can leverage regression analysis to determine which variables are either improving or hindering the production process.

The following figure summarizes Analytics Level 1:

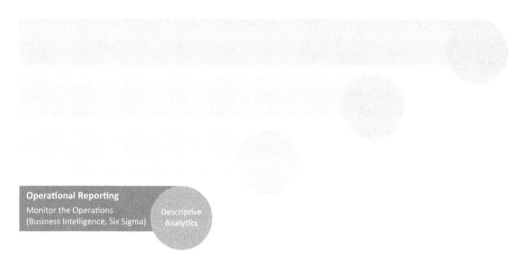

Figure 3.6: Analytics Level 1

Level 2: Insights and foresight

Level 2 seeks to identify or uncover and codify the trends, patterns, and relationships in the data and determine the strength and accuracy of those trends, patterns, and relationships. This is the foundational level for more advanced analytics.

Level 2 includes statistical analysis, data mining, and exploratory analytics (e.g., clustering, classification, and regression) to identify trends, patterns, and relationships between data elements, quantify cause and effect, determine confidence levels, and measure the Goodness of Fit concerning the strength of these trends, patterns, and relationships. Level-2 analytics sets the foundations for level-3 analytics, where we seek to predict what will happen next and then make prescriptive recommendations as to the *next best action*.

Let's discuss some building blocks for level-2 insights and foresight. I know that you would prefer to skip this section but remember it's perhaps easier to grind through these next couple of pages versus reading a 450-page academic book on statistics!

Statistical analytics

Statistics forms a foundation of all of our data science work. There are many statistical techniques and theorems, and I have found the following the most pertinent to the everyday Citizen of Data Science:

- **Probability** is a single number between 0 to 100 that is a measure of the odds or likelihood that a particular event will occur, where a number closer to 0 indicates that the event is highly unlikely to happen, while a number closer to 100 indicates that the event is highly likely to happen. Probabilities are typically expressed as percentages ranging from 0% to 100%; for example, the probability of Stephen Curry making a 3-point jump shot is 42.8%.

- **Statistics** is a branch of applied mathematics that involves collecting, classifying, analyzing, and drawing conclusions from sets of data to determine the likelihood of a specific event occurring (e.g., it raining today, winning an election, hitting a home run, or not busting when playing Blackjack). Statistics consists of the analysis of past events to support hypothesis testing and provide a level of confidence in model outcomes.

- **Statistical principles** that help us understand the strength of relationships and correlations between data elements include:

    - **Confidence levels**, indicating the trust that one should have that a particular outcome will fall within a predictable range, to measure how sure we can be about the predictability of an outcome. For example, we have 90% confidence that Stephen Curry's 3-point shooting percentage will fall within the range of 37.5% to 49.5% in any game.

    - **P-values**, used in hypothesis testing to help decide whether to reject that there is no relationship (or correlation) between your variables of interest.

    - **Goodness of Fit**, referring to a statistical test that determines how well sample data fits a distribution from a population with a normal distribution.

- **Statistical modeling** uses mathematical models and techniques to create a simplified representation of the real world by codifying trends, patterns, and relationships buried in the available data to make predictions or inferences. Statistical modeling techniques include:

    - **Time series analysis**, including **Autoregressive Integrated Moving Average (ARIMA)**, which leverages time series data to forecast future trends, exponential smoothing to analyze data with a systematic trend or seasonal component, and time series regression for predicting a future response based on historical performance.

- **Statistical forecasting**, using statistics from historical data to project what could happen in the future.

- **Bayesian statistics**, a mathematical procedure that updates probabilities to statistical problems based on new evidence or data.

Exploratory analytics

Exploratory analytics is another analytic family in level-2 analytics. Exploratory analytics refers to identifying and quantifying patterns, trends, relationships, and anomalies in data. Exploratory analytics seeks to uncover and quantify the strengths of the relationships between different data elements that can predict what's likely to happen next and make prescriptive recommendations about the next best action (level-3 advanced analytics).

Here are some standard analytic algorithms used to identify these patterns and trends:

- **Data mining** seeks to uncover statistically significant trends, patterns, and relationships buried in large data sets. Data mining is like being a detective in that it'll explore and analyze large amounts of data to uncover hidden clues in order to make better, more informed decisions. Data mining can be used in various applications, including database marketing, credit risk management, fraud detection, spam filtering, or even discerning the sentiment of users.

- **Clustering** (unsupervised machine learning) seeks to create clusters out of collections of data points that have specific shared properties or characteristics given no known relationships. The data points that belong to a particular cluster must have similar features. In contrast, the data points belonging to other clusters must be as statistically different as possible. Clustering algorithms include k-means clustering, agglomerative hierarchical clustering, divisive hierarchical clustering, and BIRCH.

- **Classification** (supervised machine learning) seeks to classify data elements with shared qualities or characteristics connected by a common, known relationship. Standard classification algorithms include logistic regression, **k-nearest neighbors** (**k-NN**), decision trees, random forest, naïve Bayes, and support vector machines.

- **Association rule** (sometimes called market basket analysis) is a rule-based machine learning method for discovering relationships of interest between data elements within or across data sets. Association rules are meant to discover the rules that determine how or why certain items are connected or appear together in the same transaction or engagement.

- **Graph analytics** seeks to determine the strength and direction of connections and patterns between entities by representing them as a graph, which is comprised of nodes (points) and edges (lines). By analyzing the resulting graph, users can discover interesting relationships, influences, and behavior between entities. Graph analytics is used in marketing, fraud detection, the supply chain, and search engine optimization.

Diagnostic analytics

Diagnostic analytics provides a report card on current operational performance. Diagnostic analytics analyzes historical data to gain insights and understand the historical behavior of a situation, which can be helpful for grading current performance and identifying areas for improvement.

Diagnostic analytics leverages BI tools and techniques, such as charts, graphs, previous period analysis, and summary statistics, to organize and present data in a meaningful way to facilitate improved diagnostic analysis.

Diagnostic analytics is also used to identify the root cause of a problem or issue. It involves using data exploration and statistical techniques to uncover the underlying causes of performance issues, trends, or anomalies in an organization's operations. The goal of diagnostic analytics is to provide detailed and actionable insights to inform decision-making and improve the overall performance of an organization.

The following figure summarizes Analytics Level 2:

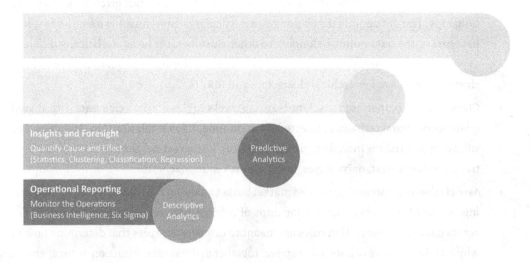

Figure 3.7: Analytics Level 2

Let's look at machine learning next as it covers such a broad range of analytic algorithms. I included some of the supervised and unsupervised machine learning algorithms – such as KNN, decision trees, clustering, and association rules – in the Level 2: Insights and Foresights analytics category. These particular machine learning algorithms are better suited to level 2 because they help us uncover insights or predicted behavioral and performance propensities that we will leverage in the level 3: Augmented Human Intelligence analytics category.

Machine learning

There are two popular types of machine learning – supervised and unsupervised machine learning – in level-2 analytics. There is a third type of machine learning, reinforcement learning, which we will cover in level 4 because reinforcement learning is the heart of autonomous analytics that powers autonomous vehicles and devices (such as vacuums and mowers) and GenAI.

Machine learning algorithms analyze, identify, and codify trends, patterns, and relationships buried in data, and subsequently use those trends, patterns, and relationships to make more accurate predictions that augment human decision-making. These algorithms are trained on large volumes of data, learning from examples and experience buried in that data. The more data the algorithms analyze, the better the algorithms become at recognizing and codifying the trends, patterns, and relationships necessary to make more accurate predictions.

The difference between supervised machine learning and unsupervised machine learning is that with supervised machine learning, we know the outcomes (labeled outcomes) and can work backward to understand the variables that influenced those outcomes. With unsupervised machine learning, we do not know the outcomes (no labeled outcomes), so the unsupervised machine learning algorithms search for similar data elements. Let's understand that in more detail:

- **Supervised machine learning** identifies *"known unknown" relationships* from labeled or known outcomes (e.g., fraud, customer attrition, purchases, and website conversions). Supervised machine learning teaches a model to make predictions or decisions by showing it examples with known answers. It learns from these examples to find patterns and make accurate predictions on new data. Supervised machine learning algorithms include KNN, decision trees, random forest, and naïve Bayes.

- **Unsupervised machine learning** identifies *"unknown unknown" relationships* from data with no known outcomes. Unsupervised machine learning discovers hidden patterns and structures in data without being given any specific answers or labels. Instead of having predefined or labeled outcomes, the unsupervised machine learning algorithms look for patterns or similarities in the data and organize it in a meaningful way. Unsupervised machine learning uses analytic algorithms such as clustering, segmentation, and association rules.

Level 3: Augmented human intelligence

Level 3 seeks to augment human intelligence by predicting what's likely to happen and recommending the next best actions to improve human decision-making effectiveness. Level 3 seeks to augment human intelligence through more informed decision-making. The third level of advanced analytics seeks to leverage the trends, patterns, and relationships uncovered and codified in level-2 analytics to predict what will happen next and then generate prescriptive recommendations and actions to improve the effectiveness of decision-making.

Categories of analytics that fall into Level 3 include neural networks (or deep learning), regression analysis (a form of supervised machine learning), recommendation engines, and federated learning. Let's look at them in a bit more detail in the upcoming sections.

Neural networks

Neural networks comprise a significant portion of level-3 analytics. A neural network contains multiple neurons that collaborate to learn to recognize patterns. For example, imagine you want to teach a neural network to recognize apples and bananas. You could create a neural network with two layers of neurons.

The first layer looks at the fruit and tries to recognize basic features, like shape and color. For example, it might notice that apples are round and red, while bananas are long and yellow. The second layer takes those features and tries to guess which fruit it is. If the first layer noticed the fruit was round and red, the second layer might predict it was an apple. And just like a human, the more the neural network is used and trained, the better it becomes at recognizing things.

There are many types of neural networks, each optimized for a different kind of analytic problem:

- **Recurrent Neural Networks (RNNs)** are neural networks with memory that allow information to flow forward and backward, creating a loop that enables the network to remember and consider previous inputs while processing current inputs. This feedback mechanism allows the network to retain information from earlier steps, making it useful for tasks that involve sequences or patterns over time, like speech recognition, language translation, or auto-completion.

- **Feed-Forward Neural Networks** are a type of artificial neural network where information flows in only one direction, from the input layer to the output layer. Each layer of the network consists of interconnected nodes that perform computations on the input data and pass the results to the next layer.

There are no feedback loops like in an RNN. Feed-forward neural networks are more like a pipeline that processes data step by step, making them ideal for processing-heavy tasks like image recognition, pattern classification, or predicting a single output based on given inputs.

- **Convolutional Neural Networks (CNNs)** are a type of artificial neural network designed to analyze and understand visual data. CNNs leverage convolutional layers to automatically learn and extract meaningful features from input images or videos. A CNN possesses a network of interconnected filters that collaborate to recognize objects, detect edges, or classify images, making it useful for applications like image classification, object detection, and image generation.

- **Generative Adversarial Networks (GANs)** consist of two competing neural networks: a generator and a discriminator. The generator tries to create new data, such as images or music, from a given data set. The discriminator tries to distinguish between the generated data and real data. The generator tries to create increasingly realistic data to fool the discriminator, while the discriminator gets better at distinguishing real and fake data in a continuous game of cat-and-mouse. GANs have enabled impressive advancements in generating realistic images and videos and are used in various applications such as art generation, deepfake detection, data augmentation, and synthetic data generation.

Regression analysis

Regression analysis seeks to codify cause-and-effect relationships found in data. Regression analysis consists of a set of statistical processes for estimating the relationships between a dependent variable (often called the *outcome* or *response* variable, or a *label* in machine learning parlance) and one or more independent variables (often called *predictors*, *covariates*, *explanatory variables*, or *features*). There are many regression analysis algorithms, the most common being linear regression and multivariate regression:

- **Linear regression** analyzes the relationship between two variables by fitting a straight line to a set of data points. It quantifies how changes in one variable impact the other variable, enabling users to make predictions based on this relationship. By finding the line that minimizes the differences between the observed data points and the predicted values, linear regression provides a simple yet powerful way to model and quantify the association between two variables.

- **Multivariate regression** analyzes the relationship between multiple independent variables and a single dependent variable. Multivariate regression quantifies how changes in multiple variables collectively contribute to the changes in the dependent variable. By estimating the coefficients for each independent variable, multivariate regression enables us to quantify their individual contributions and assess their significance in predicting the outcome variable, such as the impact that income level, education level, age, gender, and marital status might have on influencing your decision to buy a particular vehicle.

Recommendation engines

Recommendation engines analyze a history of transactions and engagement data to make suggestions or recommendations to a specific user, such as a book, a video, or a job. Recommendation engines are widely used to provide personalized suggestions and recommendations to users in various business functions including e-commerce, streaming services, social media connections, travel, entertainment, and content distribution.

Collaborative filtering is the most common technique used when building recommender systems. Collaborative filtering matches items a particular user might like based on the preferences and actions of a similar set of users or cohorts. Collaborative filtering analyzes the purchase and engagement history of a large group of users to identify small clusters of *like* users with similar tastes or preferences. It then looks at the items that those *like* users prefer to create a ranked list of suggestions for a particular user. For example, suppose a group of customers who are similar to me enjoy a specific movie, restaurant, or book. In that case, the recommender system will recommend that movie, restaurant, or book to me.

Content-based filtering is another recommendation engine example that recommends items to users based on their previous preferences and engagement activities. It analyzes the features or attributes of items that the user has liked or bought and suggests similar items. For example, if a user has shown interest in Arnold Schwarzenegger movies, a content-based filtering engine would recommend other action movies based on similar genres or plot similarities (expect a steady stream of *Predator*, *Commando*, and *Terminator* movie recommendations).

Federated learning

Federated learning trains an algorithm across multiple decentralized devices without the requirement to first exchange or share the data. Federated learning enables distributed devices (mobile phones, autonomous vehicles, telco switches) to collaboratively train a shared prediction model while keeping all the training data on each device. A device downloads the current model, improves the model via training from its data, summarizes the model improvements, and shares only the model improvements with a centralized repository where all the improvements are integrated to improve the shared model. This approach accelerates the ability to share learning across devices, mitigates potentially enormous transaction costs by only transmitting model updates, and avoids issues with data localization laws.

 Data localization laws are legislation that dictates the permissible processing of data within a specific jurisdiction. It is important to distinguish data localization from data sovereignty, as the latter pertains to the hosting of data in a particular country and subjects it to the corresponding country or state laws.

Common applications of federated learning include:

- In healthcare, hospitals or medical institutions can collaborate using federated learning to train a predictive model on patient data without sharing sensitive patient data.

- In IoT, federated learning can be used to improve performance or enable new functionalities for IoT devices. For example, smart thermostats from different homes can collaborate to learn energy usage patterns collectively while keeping individual user data private.

- Banks and financial institutions can utilize federated learning to develop fraud detection models without sharing customers' transaction details.

- For autonomous vehicles, instead of transmitting sensitive data from individual vehicles to a central server, each vehicle can learn locally and contribute model updates to improve the overall driving experience, traffic prediction, or obstacle detection.

- In edge computing, federated learning can be used to train models on distributed devices without transmitting the raw data to the cloud, thereby reducing bandwidth usage and latency while ensuring data privacy.

The following figure summarizes Analytics Level 3:

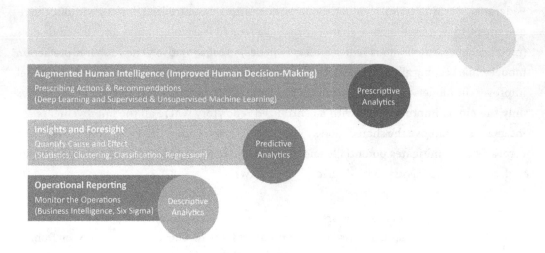

Figure 3.8: Analytics Level 3

Level 4: Autonomous analytics

Level 4 seeks to create autonomous or semi-autonomous analytics-driven assets (products, devices, policies, procedures, processes) that can continuously learn and adapt as they interact with their environment with minimal human intervention. The fourth level of advanced analytics is the holy grail of analytics maturity. It represents an accumulation of data and analytic capabilities gathered as organizations navigate the Analytics Maturity Index to create semi-autonomous analytics.

This is the area of advanced analytics that holds the most potential to dramatically improve user experiences and optimize operational performance. Level-4 analytics are fundamentally different from the previous three levels as these analytics are focused on learning and adapting within an ever-changing environment versus optimizing within a given environment. This is also the area causing the most concern among regulators and politicians because of the ability of level-4 analytics to learn and adapt more quickly than laws and regulations can be created and enforced to govern their responsible and ethical use.

Reinforcement learning

Reinforcement learning is a powerful machine learning algorithm that seeks to continuously learn and adapt as it interacts with its environment. Reinforcement learning seeks to maximize rewards while minimizing costs or penalties as it interacts with its environment. Reinforcement learning uses trial-and-error techniques to map situations to actions to maximize rewards and minimize costs, like how the children's game of *Hot and Cold* is played.

One challenge of reinforcement learning is that actions not only affect immediate rewards and penalties but actions may also affect subsequent or longer-term rewards and penalties. So, an evaluation of the full extent of rewards and penalties must be considered when measuring reinforcement learning effectiveness (hint: this is key).

Reinforcement learning is trained by replaying a particular situation (playing a video game, vacuuming the house, or driving a car) millions of times. The program is rewarded when it makes a good decision and given no reward (or punished) when it loses or makes a wrong decision. The resulting rewards and punishments lead to adjustments in the weights of the model's variables and metrics to influence the model to make the *right* moves without programmers having to explicitly program the rules into the game.

For example, ChatGPT uses a combination of supervised machine learning (with known or labeled outcomes) and **Reinforcement Learning with Human Feedback (RLHF)** as it interacts with its users to continuously learn and adapt its AI models, which seek to optimize the matching of relevant content to the user's request. The ChatGPT *thumbs-up* button tells the ChatGPT AI model that it generated the right outcome, while the *thumbs-down* button tells the model that it did not generate the right outcome (and provides an opportunity for the human to provide feedback, which ChatGPT uses to learn and adapt).

As reinforcement learning algorithms become increasingly integrated into commercial and industrial products, it is important to establish guidelines to prevent these products or devices from inadvertently adopting behaviors that could harm humans. That includes:

- **Articulating the reward structure**: Development teams need to thoroughly research, comprehend, build, and validate the rewards that reinforcement learning will aim to optimize. For example, suppose you are a social media network that builds an AI model that only seeks to optimize clicks, likes, and shares. In that case, your AI model will likely yield AI confirmation bias and eventually inhibit the growth of your customer base since you will only reach out to the same customers you already have.

- **Codifying the cost structure**: Development teams must also understand and quantify the costs and punishments thoroughly. This includes exploring a robust and comprehensive set of operational scenarios to ensure that one has thoroughly captured the potential second- and third-order costs, including the costs associated with false positives and false negatives. Returning to our social media network example, this would include understanding and quantifying the costs associated with not providing more diverse content to reach and acquire new customers.

Reinforcement learning is the heart of AI, a topic that we will explore in depth in the next chapter.

Generative AI

Generative AI (GenAI) is a type of AI that can generate new content – such as text, images, photos, poems, or music – based on learning from existing works. This can be done using various techniques such as machine learning algorithms or neural networks. GenAI models are trained on large amounts of data and use statistical methods to generate outputs similar to the data they were trained on but not exact copies.

OpenAI's ChatGPT is an example of GenAI. ChatGPT is a conversational AI model developed by OpenAI, which uses deep learning algorithms to generate human-like text responses based on the input it receives. While ChatGPT can generate text similar to human language, it cannot understand or learn the same way a human can. Other GenAI chatbots include Google Bard and Microsoft Bing.

We will do a deeper dive into GenAI in *Chapter 10*, discussing how it works and understanding some of its key enabling technologies.

Artificial General Intelligence

Artificial General Intelligence (AGI) is an AI that can perform a wide range of tasks and functions at a level equivalent to or surpassing human intelligence. In other words, AGI replicates human intelligence by possessing the capability to think, comprehend, acquire knowledge, and apply its intelligence to effectively solve problems equal to or surpassing human capabilities in any given situation.

At the time of writing this book, AGI does not exist. Current AI systems are limited in generalizing and adapting to new situations outside of their specific domain or training data. They are designed to excel at particular tasks but lack the flexibility and creativity that humans possess—sorry, *Terminator* fanboys.

AGI is an aspirational long-term goal that requires significant advancements in several fields, including machine learning, natural language processing, and behavioral science. Some folks believe AGI could be real within the next few decades, while others believe that it may never be possible. The encouraging news is that the growing awareness of the opportunities and risks associated with AI will hopefully prepare humans for the day when AGI is a reality.

The following figure summarizes Analytics Level 4:

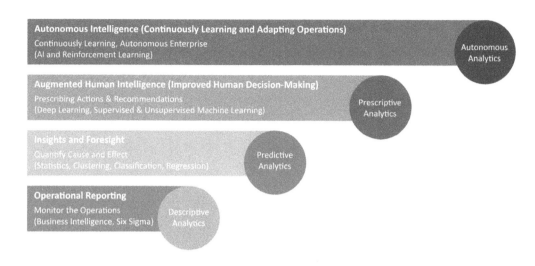

Figure 3.9: Analytics Level 4

An understanding of these four levels of analytics and where and how best to use them positions a Citizen of Data Science to proactively participate in the ideation and exploration of the best analytics to use for business and operational use cases. This truly turns the Citizen of Data Science into a valuable, contributing partner of the data science team.

Summary

While you may never be asked to program a neural network or an unsupervised machine learning algorithm, Citizens of Data Science must have a rough idea of how these algorithms work and what these algorithms are good at doing. Hopefully, the chapter helped to demystify data science and advanced analytics and provided a foundation for everyone to feel comfortable and empowered to participate in these analytics conversations.

Finally, there is a dramatic conceptual difference between level-3 and level-4 analytics. The primary goal of level-3 analytics is to help improve, or optimize, human decision-making. However, level-4 analytics introduces an entirely new concept with learning analytics – analytics that can learn and adapt with minimal human intervention.

The next chapter will focus on understanding how AI works and the critical role of the AI utility function in guiding an AI model's workings. I will also explain the vital role that you as humans play in defining a healthy and responsible AI utility function.

Join our book's Discord space

Join our Discord community to meet like-minded people and learn alongside more than 4000 people at:

https://packt.link/data

4

Understanding How AI Works

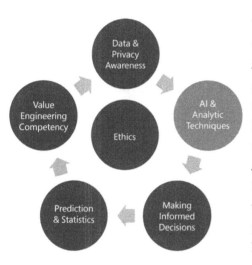

The previous chapter introduced us to the world of analytics, including key analytic concepts and the Analytics Maturity Index. But AI is too much of a game-changer to not be given its own chapter. AI is different from any other analytics technology we have seen. Unlike traditional analytics that seek to optimize operational use cases, AI seeks to learn. And AI can continuously learn and adapt at speeds billions if not trillions of times faster than humans with minimal human intervention; without the proper precautions and AI model training, that can lead to disastrous unintended consequences.

So, let's use this chapter to deep dive into how AI works and the vital role that every person needs to play in defining the AI utility function that guides how the AI model works to achieve user-defined outcomes.

This chapter will cover the following topics:

- How does AI work?
- What constitutes a healthy AI utility function?
- How to optimize AI-based learning systems

How does AI work?

An AI model is a set of algorithms that seeks to optimize decisions and actions by mapping probabilistic outcomes to a utility value within a constantly changing environment...with minimal human intervention.

 Utility value describes the subjective value the AI model assigns to different outcomes based on its programmed goals and objectives. For example, an AI designed to maximize profit for a company may assign a higher utility value to decisions that result in increased revenue or decreased expenses. In comparison, an AI designed to improve healthcare outcomes may assign a higher utility value to decisions that lead to improved patient outcomes and reduced healthcare costs.

This set of algorithms can learn trends, patterns, and relationships buried in data and make predictions based on those trends, patterns, and relationships to make decisions and act on them. The AI model is trained on a data set consisting of variables and metrics (input data) that corresponds to specific outcomes (output data). Then during production, the AI model constantly adjusts the weights associated with those variables and metrics to minimize the difference between its predicted and actual outcomes.

AI is quite a simple concept. AI is like the children's game of Hotter–Colder, where a child is seeking to find a hidden present, and the only feedback that they are given is whether they are getting hotter (moving closer to the present) or colder (moving further from the present). The only difference between AI and the Hotter–Colder game is that the present is constantly moving in the AI world.

The AI model is trained and continuously learns and adapts to pursue its desired outcomes using the following process:

1. The Data Science team and the subject-matter experts collaborate to define the AI utility function, including the variables, metrics, weights (priorities), and outcome utility value that the AI model will use to guide its decisions and actions.

2. The AI model interacts with its environment, making decisions and taking actions based on the variables, metrics, and associated weights in the AI utility function.

3. The AI model receives feedback on the effectiveness of its decisions and actions (analyzing the difference between predicted versus actual outcomes).

4. The AI model tweaks the AI utility function weights and outcome utility value based on the decision effectiveness feedback so that the AI model can continue to minimize the difference between predicted and actual outcomes.

The AI model uses two techniques to guide the direction and size of tweaks that are made to the weights that comprise the AI utility function:

- **Backpropagation** improves the accuracy of AI model predictions by gradually adjusting the weights of the AI utility function variables until the predicted results match the actual results. Technically, backpropagation computes the gradient of the loss function with respect to the model parameters, representing the direction of the maximum loss reduction.

- **Stochastic Gradient Descent (SGD)** is an optimization algorithm that uses the gradients computed by backpropagation to update the AI utility function weights to reduce the loss defined by the AI utility function. Technically, SGD seeks to minimize the cost function by iteratively moving toward the steepest descent defined by the negative gradient (slope).

Backpropagation and SGD allow the AI model to adjust the weights in the AI utility function to minimize the loss function by finding the variable and metric weights that produce the best performance for a desired outcome, as can be seen in the following figure:

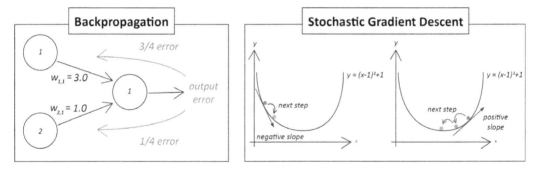

Figure 4.1: Role of backpropagation and SGD

One of the best real-world examples of AI in action is the Roomba® 900 iRobot® vacuum. The Roomba® 900 iRobot® vacuum leverages streaming data from on-board sensors and a low-resolution camera to ingest and analyze a steady stream of data about its operating environment, which its AI utility function uses to guide how the vacuum navigates through a room to clean it effectively and efficiently.

The Roomba® 900 iRobot® traverses the house, identifies and remembers obstacles (landmarks), and remembers which routes work best to clean the house. It builds a map of the house and uses each vacuuming excursion to refine and update that map.

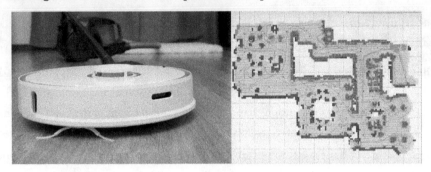

Figure 4.2: Roomba® 900 iRobot® continuously learns and adapts to its environment

In the next section, we will discuss the AI utility function, which plays an important role in shaping the AI model's operational effectiveness. Since AI systems are dumb systems that only seek to optimize around the variables, metrics, weights, and the outcome utility value defined in the AI utility function, defining the AI utility function holistically and comprehensively becomes critical.

What constitutes a healthy AI utility function?

The **AI utility function** is a set of factors (variables and metrics) with associated weights that map outcomes to utility values to guide an AI model's decision-making process. It measures decision effectiveness and continuously learns and adapts to improve performance. It is a mathematical expression that maps the input space (e.g., the possible actions an AI model can take) against a set of output values representing the operating environment's preferences or goals. The weights assigned to different variables and metrics determine the relative importance of those variables and metrics in the AI model's decision-making process. By maximizing the expected utility of its decisions, an AI model can make choices more likely to achieve the desired operational outcomes.

An AI model will continuously seek to optimize its AI utility function as the AI model interacts with its operating environment. The AI model provides positive and negative feedback to the AI utility function so that the AI utility function can learn and adapt the weights of the variables and metrics that comprise the AI utility function to make the *right* decisions and actions.

To make the *right* decisions and actions that maximize the expected utility:

- The AI utility function develops a probabilistic model to estimate the likelihood of different states or outcomes based on the available information.

- The AI model then uses a variety or combination of advanced analytic algorithms and techniques, such as supervised learning and reinforcement learning, to learn from labeled or known outcomes, to continuously update and adjust the AI utility function.

The role of the AI utility function involves the following steps:

1. Capture the variables, metrics, and associated weights we want to guide the AI model's actions.

2. Employ those variables, metrics, and associated weights to guide the AI model as it takes actions and makes decisions.

3. Capture the results and effectiveness of those actions (predicted versus actual outcomes).

4. Update the variables, metrics, and associated weights in the AI utility function based on the results of those actions.

AI Models Seek to Continuously Learn and Adapt to Its Environment

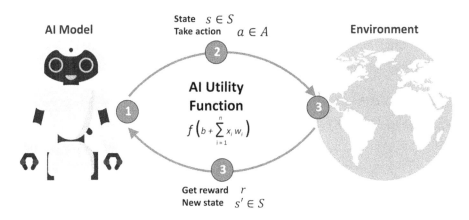

Figure 4.3: AI utility function guides AI models' decisions and actions

For example, in a self-driving car, the AI model can use on-board sensors, cameras, and LiDAR to estimate the location and speed of nearby vehicles and then use a probabilistic model to estimate the likelihood of different outcomes (e.g., whether a nearby vehicle will change lanes or maintain its current path).

LiDAR, which stands for Light Detection and Ranging, is a detection system that uses light in the form of a pulsed laser to measure ranges. LiDAR has the ability to calculate incredibly accurate distances to many objects that are simultaneously detected – a big advantage over cameras.

Tight collaboration between a diverse set of stakeholders and subject-matter experts to brainstorm, validate, and prioritize the variables and metrics that comprise the AI utility function in the context of the outcomes we are trying to achieve is not just critical, it's mandatory. Defining these variables and metrics too narrowly can lead to AI model confirmation bias and potentially dangerous unintended consequences. We will discuss how to drive organizational alignment and consensus on the targeted business or operational opportunity in *Chapter 6*.

The entire concept and process of AI are based upon continuous learning and adapting to create value. But value is a nebulous concept, and not properly and comprehensively defining value at the beginning of the AI process is a great way to ensure project failure – not failure to make the AI models work, but failure to deliver meaningful, relevant, responsible, and ethical outcomes. As popular, educator, author, and businessman Stephen Covey famously said, "Begin with an end in mind." And that *end* from an AI perspective starts and stops by properly defining *value*.

Defining "value"

Identifying the variables and metrics that comprise a healthy AI utility function – an AI utility function that delivers relevant, meaningful, and ethical outcomes – requires a more holistic definition of *value* beyond the traditional financial and operating variables and metrics. A healthy AI utility function should include variables from each of the following value classes:

- **Financial** variables, including return on investments, net present value, shareholder value, capital availability, and gross national product
- **Operational** variables, including reliability, predictability, repeatability, stability, safety, and scalability
- **Customer** variables, including perceived value, enjoyment, satisfaction, likelihood to recommend, net promoter, quality, safety, and fairness
- **Employee** variables, including employee productivity, satisfaction, LTR, leadership, mentoring, influencer, and catalyst

- **Partner/supplier** variables, including financial health, reliability, quality, component importance, supply chain effectiveness, production risks, management stability, **enviromental, social and governance (ESG)** efforts, diversity efforts, environment efforts
- **Societal** variables, including improving quality of life and healthcare, access to clean air and water, job creation, and education availability
- **Environment** variables, including improving energy efficiency, recycling, and sustainability while reducing the carbon footprint
- **Spiritual (ethical)** variables, including doing good, giving back, mentoring, harmony, solemn, belief, devotion, and ethics

The following figure highlights the broad range of dimensions of value that organizations must consider as they contemplate the economic impact of their AI models. It is irresponsible to just consider the obvious financial and operational value measures without giving full consideration to the other, equally important dimensions of value including employee, partners, societal, environmental, and spiritual.

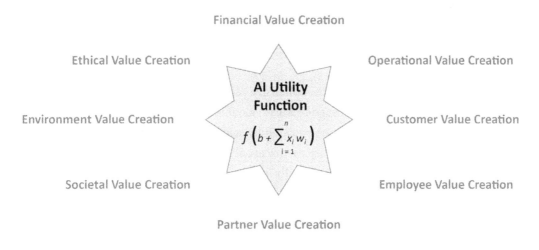

Figure 4.4: Economic value definition

In considering the variables and metrics to include in your AI utility function, it is crucial to understand and differentiate between lagging and leading indicators. It's hard to create a practical, relevant, and ethical AI utility function if the AI model is being asked to optimize on measures that measure what has already happened versus optimizing on measures that predict what is likely to happen.

Understanding leading vs. lagging indicators

Leading indicators signal future events, whereas lagging indicators present information that happens after an event. A critical factor in identifying the variables and metrics comprising a healthy AI utility function is understanding the difference between leading and lagging indicators:

- A **leading indicator** is a measure that tends to predict what is likely to happen next. In economics, leading indicators are economic metrics and statistics that tend to change *before* the overall economy changes. Economic leading indicators include the consumer confidence index, purchasing managers index, job postings, and new housing permits.

- A **lagging indicator** measures something that has already happened. In economics, lagging indicators are economic metrics and statistics that tend to change *after* the overall economy changes. They are used to confirm past economic activity. Examples of economic lagging indicators include GDP, inflation, and unemployment rate.

Leading indicators can predict the performance of lagging indicators. For example, in baseball, batting average is a lagging indicator, an after-the-fact measure of how many hits the batter gets as a percentage of at-bats. On the other hand, walks are a leading indicator of batting averages because a selective batter will only swing at pitches on which they have a high probability of hitting solidly.

In 2022, Aaron Judge had one of the best offensive seasons in baseball history and was consequently selected as the American League's Most Valuable Player. But Mr. Judge could improve his batting average (lagging indicator) by carefully selecting which pitches to swing (leading indicator). For example, developing the patience to only swing at pitches within the white strike zone in the following figure could dramatically impact his already impressive batting average:

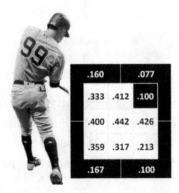

Figure 4.5: Aaron Judge's batting average by Strike Zone

One more interesting observation: Aaron Judge could improve his batting average by not swinging at pitches in the upper-right-hand corner of the strike zone, even though those pitches are strikes. The willingness to *wait for his pitches* at the expense of potentially striking out is another way that Aaron Judge could improve his AI utility function and deliver more impactful outcomes (as if he needs more help in doing such).

How to optimize AI-based learning systems

Next, we want to expand your role in driving the AI conversation by explaining the importance of first understanding or determining user intent and then discussing the importance of defining conflicting variables and metrics and how multi-objective optimization will guide the trade-off decisions and actions that the AI model must make. Let's understand this with an example!

Whether you use Google Maps, Apple Maps, or Waze (also owned by Google), these AI-infused apps are fantastic at getting you from Point A to Point B in the shortest time. They give you step-by-step directions and can update those directions based on current information (e.g., traffic accidents, weather, potholes, special events, etc.) that pop up during your trip.

Let's consider the different variables and metrics that we would want to include in the AI utility function to help the GPS optimize our journey. Two classes of variables and metrics to include in the AI utility function might be:

1. **Driver's driving preferences**, which include classes of variables and metrics such as:

    - **Road conditions**, considering current weather, road maintenance plans, road surface conditions, local events, surface composition (concrete, asphalt, gravel), last maintenance dates, etc.

    - **Route safety**, considering neighborhood crime activity, location of car accidents, the severity of car accidents, time of day, seasonality, etc.

    - **Scenic sites**, considering scenic views, museums, historical sites, etc.

2. **Vehicle operating efficiencies**, which include classes of variables and metrics such as:

    - **Miles-to-destination** to minimize wear-and-tear on the car, detours, special events or activities along the journey route, etc.

    - **Time-to-destination** to get you to your destination as quickly as possible considering historical traffic patterns, stop lights and stop signs, school zones, local events, road type (interstate versus state highways), number of lanes, speed zones, etc.

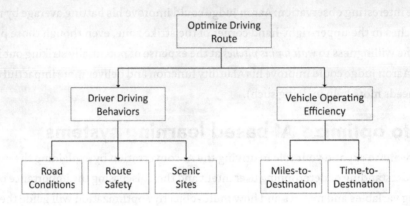

Figure 4.6: Variables, weights, and AI-power GPS optimization

Apple and Google's AI-powered GPS mapping applications are optimized to get you from Point A to Point B in the fastest possible time. But what if getting from Point A to Point B as fast as possible is not your intent? What if your travel intentions are something different? Hence, AI model effectiveness starts by thoroughly understanding user intent. That is, what is the user trying to accomplish, what are their desired outcomes, and what are the KPIs and metrics against which the user will measure success?

Understand user intent

User Intent Determination is understanding or determining what the user is trying to accomplish (their intent) so the AI model can optimize its actions and decisions to achieve the most relevant outcomes. I'm shocked at how many AI projects start without first understanding user intent.

Without first understanding user intent, it is nearly impossible to distinguish signal from noise in the data; it is almost impossible to ascertain what's valuable and not valuable in the data. The role of user intent in delivering relevant, accurate, and ethical AI outcomes can best be summarized by the following process:

- **Intent Determination**: What is the user trying to accomplish (their intent), what are their objectives and desired outcomes, and how will the user measure the effectiveness of their intent?

- **Value Definition (AI utility function)**: What are the variables, metrics (features), and associated weights against which the AI model will seek to achieve the user's desired outcomes?

- **Value Creation (AI Model)**: What actions or decisions must the AI model make to optimize the variables and metrics against which the desired outcome's success will be measured?

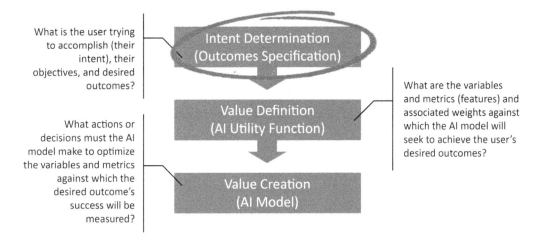

Figure 4.7: AI model optimization starts by understanding user intent

Returning to our GPS example, what if our intent isn't to get from Point A to Point B as fast as possible? What if our intent is the least expensive path (considering tolls), the safest route (considering neighborhood crimes like carjacking or traffic accidents), or the most scenic route (considering picturesque viewing options or historical sites of interest)?

The weights we assign to the variables and metrics (against which the AI model will seek to continuously optimize) would change dramatically based on our intent. This can be seen in the following figure:

Optimal Route Features	(A) Minimize Time-to-Destination	(B) Provide Safest Route	(C) Provide Scenic or Historic Site Route
Road Conditions	0.20	0.20	0.00
Route Safety	0.10	0.70	0.15
Historic Sites	0.00	0.00	0.70
Miles-to-Destination	0.00	0.10	0.00
Time-to-Destination	0.70	0.00	0.15

Figure 4.8: Changing variable weights based on the user's intent

For example, suppose we intended to get from Point A to Point B on the safest route. In that case, our weights might more heavily favor the Route Safety variables but also consider Road Conditions while minimizing miles to drive that can impact Route Safety. Or if our intent was the most scenic route, then we might want to give more weight to Historic Sites but also consider Route Safety and Time-to-Destination (as I don't want to spend a week driving all over the state visiting random sites of interest).

Based on the user's intent, our AI-fueled GPS would rebalance the weights and variables that comprise the AI utility function to yield different route recommendations, as shown in the following figure:

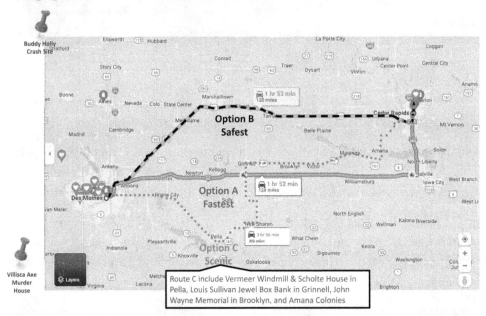

Figure 4.9: Route recommendations based on driver intent

If I had chosen Option C (Scenic) and immediately started my trip by veering toward Clear Lake, IA, to see the Buddy Holly crash site, then the AI utility would know that my time-to-destination weight was not nearly as high as initially estimated and would change the weights in the AI utility function accordingly and likely have me driving all over the state to see other potential sites of interest such as the Hart-Parr museum in Charles City and Spring Park in Osage, as shown in the following figure:

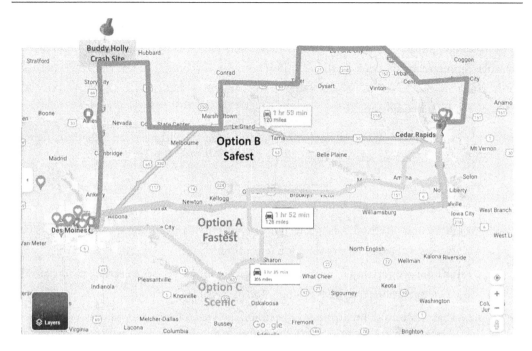

Figure 4.10: AI utility function changes AI model's recommendations based on user actions

Understanding how AI models work explains the behavior of the Terminator – the Terminator was only seeking its user's desired outcomes based on the codified and articulated sets of variables, metrics, and weights that comprised its AI utility function.

Build diversity

Multi-objective optimization (MOO) is a branch of decision-making that deals with mathematical optimization problems requiring simultaneous optimization of multiple objective functions.

AI models will access, analyze, and make decisions billions, if not trillions, of times faster than humans. An AI model will find the gaps in a poorly constructed AI utility function and will quickly exploit that gap to the potential detriment of many key stakeholders. Consequently, it is absolutely critical to create a robust AI utility function, one that incorporates conflicting variables and metrics to prompt the AI model to grapple with trade-off decisions, ultimately driving optimal outcomes. Picture a scenario where we strive to improve variable A while simultaneously reducing variable B, while also increasing variable C and optimizing variable D. This approach enables us to create AI models that can navigate the complexities of decision-making and drive meaningful, relevant, responsible, and ethical outcomes.

One way to resolve conflicting values that comprise the AI utility function is using a multi-objective optimization algorithm where the AI utility function is forced to optimize multiple conflicting variables simultaneously. That is, the AI utility function is forced to make trade-offs between conflicting variables in its decision-making in the same way that humans are forced to make trade-offs in their decision-making.

The good news is that several multi-objective optimization algorithms excel at optimizing multiple conflicting objectives. A few of them are as follows:

- **Pareto Frontier**: Creates a set of optimal solutions where no solution can be improved in one objective without sacrificing another
- **Weighted Sum Method**: Assigns weights to objectives and combines those weights into a single aggregated objective function for optimization
- **Evolutionary Algorithms**: Inspired by biological evolution, uses selection, mutation, and crossover operations to evolve a population of possible solutions
- **Constraint Method**: Incorporates constraints in the optimization problem to find solutions that satisfy multiple objectives and constraints simultaneously
- **Multi-Objective Linear Programming**: Optimizes multiple linear objectives subject to pre-defined linear constraints
- **Multi-Objective Quadratic Programming**: Optimizes multiple quadratic objectives subject to linear or quadratic constraints
- **Non-linear Programming**: Optimizes multiple non-linear objectives subject to non-linear constraints
- **Multi-Objective Tabu Search**: A metaheuristic algorithm that explores the search space to find multiple solutions by using a tabu list that avoids revisiting previously explored solutions
- **NSGA-II Multi-Objective Evolutionary Algorithm**: A popular evolutionary algorithm that uses a non-dominated sorting technique and crowding distance calculation to maintain a diverse set of solutions along the Pareto frontier

Understanding how to identify, explore, validate, and integrate conflicting variables and metrics into your AI utility function ensures that the AI models are working for our benefit in delivering meaningful, relevant, responsible, and ethical outcomes.

Just like humans are constantly forced to make difficult trade-off decisions (drive to work quickly but also arrive safely, improve the quality of healthcare while also improving the economy), we must expect nothing less from a tool like AI that can make those tough trade-off decisions without biases or prejudices.

Summary

AI is the ultimate goal of an organization's analytics maturity. AI builds upon the analytic maturity levels of operational reporting, insights and foresights, and augmented human intelligence to create autonomous analytics that power the products, services, policies, and processes that can continuously learn and adapt to the changing environment in which it operates. This continuous learning and adapting of AI-powered products, services, policies, and processes can happen with minimal human intervention, which makes it unlike any technology that we have ever seen.

To become a Citizen of Data Science, everyone must understand how AI and the AI utility function collaborate and hopefully, this chapter has helped with that. That's fundamental to participating in the AI conversation and debate. But everyone also needs to understand their role in ensuring the development of a healthy AI utility function that guides the AI model to deliver meaningful, relevant, responsible, and ethical outcomes. Yeah, that's on all of us!

In the next chapter, we are going to explore how we can leverage advanced analytics and some basic statistical techniques to create simple decision models that we can use to improve our ability to make rational, more-informed decisions.

Join our book's Discord space

Join our Discord community to meet like-minded people and learn alongside more than 4000 people at:

https://packt.link/data

5

Making Informed Decisions

This chapter is all about **decision literacy**, an awareness of how we as humans make decisions. Decision literacy involves understanding our decision-making processes with the goal of making more rational, informed decisions. It involves understanding how we assess potential decisions, explore various decision options, assess potential outcomes, and ultimately select the best or ideal course of action.

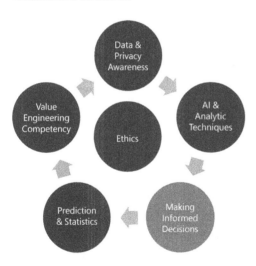

This may be the most crucial chapter in the book since the success of our personal and professional careers, not to mention the survival of our species, depends upon our ability to make informed decisions in a world of imperfect information, white lies, fake news, and alternate facts. We have already witnessed the detrimental ramifications of the lack of decision-making prowess in the COVID vaccination debates.

This chapter will start by reviewing some of the more common and deadly human decision-making traps that can skew our decisions. We'll then introduce a simple decision-making framework that anyone can employ to make more informed decisions. Finally, we'll discuss how we can think critically about the information others might use to influence our views and actions, which is critically important in an age of black-box, non-transparent, AI-powered chatbots.

Overall, we'll be discussing the following main topics in this chapter:

- Factors influencing human decisions
- 8 human decision-making traps
- Avoiding said decision-making traps
- Decision-making strategies
- Importance of critical thinking

Factors influencing human decisions

Our personal and professional success depends upon our ability to make intelligent, informed decisions. In fact, our survival as a species depends on our ability to make smart, informed decisions: decisions about whether to wear a biking helmet, get a vaccination, drive after an alcoholic drink, or when and where to swim. Our lives consist of an endless parade of decisions that we humans need to make intelligently and safely. Unfortunately, the human mind is not wired to make rational, informed decisions, and several factors impact our ability to process data to make informed decisions, including:

- **Status**: Humans have an emotional need to feel valued. A natural or *perceived* reduction in status will trigger a threat response, often at a subconscious level.
- **Certainty**: We are biologically wired to fear situations where we can't predict and prepare for different outcomes. Consequently, change initiatives, by their very nature, create uncertainty, fear, and anxiety.
- **Autonomy**: We need to feel we have a choice in what is happening. If people think they are being coerced, they get resentful, become resistant, and try to undermine the change in their peer groups.
- **Relatedness**: We are social creatures who strongly desire connection and belonging. Disruption of the relationships and networks people have worked to establish and nurture can create feelings of isolation, alienation, and marginalization.
- **Fairness**: We have biological wiring that creates powerful emotional responses to fair and unfair treatment. A real or *perceived* action of unfairness will trigger an aversive reaction, feelings of victimization, and a desire to discredit the process.

The good news is that humans can do many simple things to make more intelligent, informed decisions. To make smarter and well-informed decisions, it is essential for us to recognize and understand the inherent pitfalls and cognitive biases that can affect our decision-making processes. If we understand these human decision-making traps, then we have a greatly improved opportunity to avoid or overcome them.

Human decision-making traps

The human brain is a poor decision-making tool. Through evolution, the human brain became very good at pattern recognition and extrapolation: from "That looks like just a harmless log behind that patch of grass" to "Oops, that looks like an antelope!" to "YIKES, that's actually a saber-toothed tiger." Human survival depended upon our ability to recognize patterns and making quick, survival decisions based on those patterns.

While great at pattern recognition, unfortunately, humans are lousy number crunchers. Because of our instinctive poor number-crunching capabilities, humans depended upon heuristics, gut feel, rules of thumb, anecdotal information, and intuition as decision-making tools. But these decision models are insufficient in a real-time world where the volume, variety, and velocity of data are exploding. One only needs to travel to Las Vegas and watch how those glamorous casinos exploit our ingrained decision-making flaws to their financial advantage.

> **Trap #1:** Over-confidence bias
>
> **Trap #2:** Anchoring bias
>
> **Trap #3:** Risk aversion
>
> **Trap #4:** Sunk costs
>
> **Trap #5:** Framing
>
> **Trap #6:** Bandwagon effect
>
> **Trap #7:** Confirmation bias
>
> **Trap #8:** Decisions based on averages

Figure 5.1: Human decision-making flaws and biases

Let's review a few common human decision-making traps of which every Citizen of Data Science must be aware. Understanding these human decision-making traps is critical for raising our AI and data literacy IQ and avoiding these decision traps that can lead us to make suboptimal, incorrect, or even fatal decisions.

Trap #1: Over-confidence bias

We tend to heavily rely on our existing knowledge, often disregarding the importance of what we don't know. Overconfidence bias manifests when we mistakenly assess our abilities, intelligence, or expertise to be greater than they truly are, specifically in relation to a particular subject.

An example of overconfidence bias can be observed when organizations or individuals place excessive confidence in their experience within a particular market while venturing into a new market or introducing a product in a different category. In such cases, they may fail to conduct thorough research and analysis to understand the decision-making factors, competitive landscape, and market risks associated with the new market or product category. This overvaluation of their existing knowledge can lead to misjudgments and overlooking of crucial factors, potentially resulting in unfavorable outcomes.

Trap #2: Anchoring bias

Anchoring bias refers to a cognitive bias where individuals rely heavily on an initial piece of information or "anchor" when making decisions or judgments. This initial information often influences subsequent assessments, even if it may be arbitrary or irrelevant to the decision at hand. The anchor acts as a reference point that individuals use to evaluate and compare other information or options. Anchoring bias can lead to individuals being overly influenced by the initial reference point, resulting in skewed judgments and potentially leading to suboptimal decision-making.

For example, humans struggle to decide when to sell a stock. If someone buys a stock at $20 and then sees it rise to $80, they have a hard time selling the stock when it starts to drop because we've been anchored by the $80 price, even though they only paid $20 for that stock.

Anchoring bias is related to **Brandolini's law**, which states that the effort required to debunk misinformation is significantly higher than the effort required to create it. Brandolini's law highlights the challenge of combating misinformation and the disproportionate impact it can have on public perception, as debunking falsehoods often demands more time, resources, and effort. And this is a big problem in the age of social media, where it is so easy to state and propagate lies, half-truths, and fake news.

Trap #3: Risk aversion

Our risk tolerance is highly inconsistent. Risk aversion manifests people's general preference for certainty over uncertainty and minimizing the magnitude of the worst possible outcomes to which they are exposed. Risk aversion surfaces in the reluctance of a person to accept a bargain with an uncertain payoff rather than another deal with a more certain, but possibly lower, expected payoff.

For example, a risk-averse investor might choose to put their money into a savings account with a low but guaranteed interest rate rather than put their money into a stock that may have high expected returns but involves a chance of losing value or even the total loss of the capital.

Trap #4: Sunk costs

Sunk costs are the costs that have already been incurred and cannot be recoverable. These costs are essentially *sunk* or irretrievable. When making decisions, it is important to recognize that sunk costs hold no relevance in the decision process because these costs are not reversible or retrievable.

Unfortunately, it is common for individuals to factor in the time, money, or effort they have already invested in a decision. However, making decisions with the intention of *recovering* costs that are not retrievable can lead to irrational decision-making. Once time is spent or money is invested, it becomes impossible to recapture the expended time or reverse the money already spent.

For instance, individuals will often watch a movie in the movie theater to the end, even though they do not enjoy the movie, simply because they have already paid for it. However, the price of the movie becomes a sunk cost once the movie has started. Whether or not you enjoy the movie, the money spent on it is non-recoverable. People would rather waste their valuable time sitting till the end of a movie that they do not enjoy instead of walking out and spending that extra time doing something they enjoy. That's right, sunk costs can lead to irrational decisions.

Trap #5: Framing

How a decision is stated or framed can impact what decision is made. Framing refers to the way in which information or options are presented, emphasizing certain aspects while downplaying or omitting others. Framing can be used to highlight benefits, risks, emotions, or biases, ultimately impacting the decision-making process and outcomes.

Individuals tend to make inconsistent choices, depending on whether the question is framed to concentrate on losses or gains. For example, imagine you're a doctor, and you have to present two options to a patient for treating a medical condition:

- Option A: If you undergo surgery, there is a 90% chance of survival.
- Option B: If you don't undergo surgery, there is a 10% chance of death.

Even though both options present the same information, people often react differently to them because of how the information is framed. Option A frames the situation in terms of survival with a positive outcome, while option B frames it in terms of death with a negative outcome. This can lead to different decisions, even though the information is the same.

Trap #6: Bandwagon effect

The bandwagon effect refers to the tendency of individuals to adopt or follow a particular belief, behavior, or choice simply because others are doing the same. It's a phenomenon where people are influenced by the popularity or prevalence of a certain idea or action rather than considering it objectively.

The bandwagon effect is a cognitive bias that causes individuals to conform to a group's behaviors, beliefs, or attitudes to fit in or be perceived as normal. This can lead to a situation where a trend, opinion, or behavior gains momentum through the collective action of many vocal people.

The bandwagon effect is closely related to the FOMO – Fear of Missing Out – effect. FOMO creates anxiety that a once-in-a-lifetime opportunity may unfold and that you will miss out by not acting or being part of it. The rampant spread of news and opinions on social media can fuel FOMO.

For example, many folks jumped into cryptocurrency because of the press and opinions of so-called "experts" that this was a once-in-a-lifetime opportunity to profit from a significant financial industry disruption. And the results were, well, less than promised.

Trap #7: Confirmation bias

Confirmation bias is the tendency to seek out, interpret, and remember information in a way that confirms one's preexisting beliefs while downplaying or ignoring information that contradicts them. Confirmation bias can hinder objective decision-making by creating a skewed perception of reality, reinforcing existing beliefs, and limiting exposure to alternative perspectives or information that may challenge those beliefs.

For example, consider a person who firmly believes that human activities do not cause climate change. That person may actively seek information supporting that belief while disregarding or dismissing scientific studies that suggest otherwise. This can lead to a situation where they are heavily biased toward accepting information confirming their belief and rejecting information that contradicts it.

AI model confirmation bias is the tendency of an AI model to identify, interpret, and present recommendations in a way that confirms or supports the AI model's pre-existing assumptions. AI model confirmation bias feeds upon itself, creating an echo chamber effect concerning the biased data that continuously feeds the AI models. This is a topic we will explore in more detail in *Chapter 6*.

Trap #8: Decisions based on averages

Another less explored human decision-making trap is the tendency to rely on averages to help us make more informed decisions. If you make decisions based on averages, at best, you'll get average results. Beware of making decisions based on averages because one can drown in a river with an average depth of only 6 inches.

The challenge with making decisions based on averages is that no one is average. For example, the United States Air Force pilots were struggling to effectively command their fighter jets in the 1950s. The problem was that the cockpit had a standard design based on the 1920s average pilot. The Air Force decided to update their measurement of the average pilot and adjust the cockpit design accordingly[3].

Air Force Lieutenant Gilbert Daniels measured more than 4,000 pilots across 10 size dimensions to create an updated standard cockpit design. However, contrary to the assumption that most pilots would fall within the average range across these 10 dimensions, the findings revealed an unexpected result. Out of the 4,000 pilots surveyed, none of them were found to be within the average range across all 10 dimensions.

The Air Force's *aha* moment? If the cockpit was designed for the average pilot, it was actually designed for no pilot.

Todd Rose, the CEO of Populace and best-selling author of *The End of Average,* came up with the Jaggedness Principle of individuality[4]. The Jaggedness Principle states that when assessing a range of characteristics across a significant number of individuals, half of the individuals will possess traits that are above average while the other half will exhibit traits that are below average for a specific characteristic. Unfortunately, when considering all traits collectively, it is rare for anyone to actually possess an average level across all of them.

Since no one is *average,* why do organizations continue to make decisions based on averages? We have been taught to make decisions based on averages – average churn rate, average click rate, average market basket size, average mortality rates, and average COVID-19 death rates. And maybe when the data analytics tool of choice was a spreadsheet, the best we could do was use averages to make decisions. Unfortunately, using averages to make decisions results in overly generalized decisions that, at best, yield average results. But the world is changing rapidly as leading organizations start to use granular data to transition from making decisions based on averages to decisions based on an individual entity's predicted behavioral and performance propensities. They are moving into the world of nanoeconomics, a topic that we will explore in *Chapter 7.*

Avoiding decision-making traps

The key is to guide, not stifle, that natural human intuition that is important in identifying those variables and metrics that might be better predictors of performance and critical elements to the AI utility function. Think guard rails, not railroad tracks, in terms of how we nurture human intuition while protecting ourselves from those nasty human decision-making traps.

Here are some things that you can do to avoid falling into those decision-making traps:

- **Use analytic models**: Leverage validated statistical tools and techniques to improve the understanding of probabilities. Employ a structured analytic discipline that captures and weighs risks and opportunities. Analytic models help decision makers to understand and quantify both the decision opportunities and risks, identifying and quantifying the costs of being wrong.

- **Use the right metrics**: Confirm and then reconfirm that you are using appropriate metrics (think of the baseball analytics book *Moneyball* and how Billy Beane transformed the game of baseball by identifying more predictive leading indicators of on-field success). Just because a particular metric has always been appropriate in the past, don't assume it is suitable for your specific decision.

- **Challenge the model's assumptions**: It's important to understand the vulnerability of a model to the underlying assumptions that were used to create the model. We can use analytic techniques such as sensitivity analysis[1] (assessing how changes to certain factors affect a model's outcomes) and Monte Carlo[2] (a simulation technique that codifies the effects of variability) to understand the model vulnerabilities. For example, challenging the assumption that housing prices would never decline would have lessened the 2008 mortgage market meltdown.

- **Embrace diversity**: Seek out a wide variety of opinions and perspectives when you vet a model. Avoid *group-think* (another decision-making flaw). Have someone play the contrarian and challenge the model and its underlying assumptions. Use facilitation techniques in the decision-making process to ensure that all voices are heard, and all views are considered.

- **Carefully frame the decisions**: Let's assume you come into this process with your mind already made up (i.e., to validate a decision that you have already made). In this scenario, you will be more inclined to consume and gather data that supports your position and perhaps even fabricate reasons to ignore data that runs counter to your position. If you have a vested interest in the outcome of a particular decision, your objectivity is inevitably threatened, and the results of your analysis will most likely be biased.

- **Beware of sunk costs**: Create business models that properly treat sunk costs. Ensure that the model and analysis only consider incremental costs. And be sure that your models also include opportunity costs.

- **Measure and learn**: Use post-decision review boards and formal debriefs to capture the effectiveness of your decisions, as well as the relative effectiveness of the models and their underlying assumptions that supported those decisions, identifying both what worked (successes) and what did not work (failures) along with their underlying reasons.

- **Consider compensation factors**: Beware of counter-intuitive compensation. That is, understand how people will get paid or make money based on the decision. Money tends to skew rationale, and humans are revenue-optimization machines.

- **Leverage design thinking**: Employ design-thinking techniques and tools that challenge you to reframe, try, fail, learn, and try again when making decisions. Design thinking encourages us to empathize more with our stakeholders, define problems more clearly and holistically, generate more ideas without judgment, and gather and validate user feedback through prototyping and testing.

Exploring decision-making strategies

Now that we understand the different challenges that we humans face in making rational decisions, we need a decision-making framework that we can use to leverage data and analytics to make more informed decisions.

In the next few sections, we will introduce three decision-making frameworks – a simple decision matrix, the more advanced Pugh matrix, and the real-time OODA decision loop. You should choose the decision-making framework that's most appropriate for your context, given the costs and risks of the decision that you are trying to make.

Informed decision-making framework

Whether we know it or not, everyone creates a *model* to guide their decisions. Humans naturally develop models to support their decisions, whether it's decisions about deciding what route to take home from work, what to pick up at the grocery store, or how to pitch to a power baseball hitter like Mike Trout.

The comprehensive nature of one's decision model depends upon the importance of the decision and the costs associated with making a wrong decision. For simplicity reasons, we'll classify decisions as either low impact or high impact depending upon the costs and ramifications of making a bad decision:

- **Class 1: Low-impact decisions**

    For decisions that are low impact concerning the costs and ramifications associated with making a wrong decision, we can use *rules of thumb* or heuristics to support decisions such as changing the oil in your car every 3,000 miles, seeing a dentist every six months, or changing your undergarments at least once a day.

- **Class 2: High-impact decisions**

    For high-impact decisions (e.g., buying a house, buying a car, getting vaccinated, wearing seat belts, driving after drinking), we could build more extensive models by gathering a wide variety of relevant data sources and assessing the potential outcomes (including possible unintended consequences) to make an intelligent, informed decision.

The following figure shows a decision-making framework that anyone can use when faced with the challenge of making a high-impact decision:

Figure 5.2: Informed decision-making framework

The decision-making framework should be used for *class-2 decisions* to ensure we have considered as many options and potential outcomes as possible given the high impact costs and ramifications of making a wrong decision. The decision-making framework is comprised of the following steps:

1. **Identity and triage decision to be made**: The starting point for the decision-making process is to create a simple hypothesis around which we seek to make a decision. Clearly state the conclusion you are trying to make and identify the KPIs and metrics against which decision progress, success, and effectiveness will be measured.

2. **Create a decision matrix**: Construct a decision matrix that maps actions to potential outcomes and helps us identify the costs and ramifications of the different decision options. We'll discuss the decision matrix in more detail later in the chapter.

3. **Research and gather credible data**: Next, you want to identify, research, and gather the data necessary to support your decision. Assessing the credibility and reliability of your data sources can be challenging when researching and collecting data for the decision matrix. A careful and objective assessment of each data source is necessary as the inclusion of each data source into the analysis must be defendable.

4. **Create a cost-benefit assessment**: Performing a thorough cost-benefit assessment is crucial, particularly when dealing with decisions that carry significant ramifications. This step entails identifying both the direct and indirect costs as well as the benefits associated with each cell of the decision matrix. By carefully evaluating these factors, you can gain a comprehensive understanding of the potential advantages and drawbacks associated with each decision option.

5. **Explore worst-case scenarios**: Give due consideration to exploring worst-case scenarios, which is especially critical when building AI models. Evaluate the potential ramifications associated with making a bad or inaccurate decision. By thoroughly assessing these potential risks, you can better understand the potential downsides and make a more informed decision.

6. **Create a clear presentation**: Construct data visualizations and graphics that effectively communicate the results and findings from the assessment. By creating visually engaging and informative materials, you can enhance the understanding and clarity of the assessment, facilitating the decision-making process.

Again, this process should not lead to analysis paralysis as the speed and depth to which you follow this informed decision-making framework depend highly on the costs and ramifications of making a wrong decision.

 Special consideration is required to identify and understand the unintended consequences of your decisions. We will spend more time discussing how to identify and assess the impact of unintended consequences in *Chapter 8*.

Decision matrix

One can use different types of decision matrices to aid the decision-making process. The choice of which matrix to use depends upon the importance of the decision and the consequences of making the wrong decision.

A decision matrix is a tool used to evaluate the potential options or alternatives based on a pre-determined set of criteria. It is a structured approach to decision-making that helps individuals or teams weigh the pros and cons of each option and make a rational, informed choice. A decision matrix typically includes a list of options or alternatives, a list of criteria that are important to the decision, and a rating for each option against each criterion. The ratings are then used to calculate a total score for each option, which can be used to compare and rank the alternatives. This can help identify the best option based on the essential criteria for the decision.

For example, let's say that we are trying to decide between four different movies for our evening viewing pleasure:

- Movie 1 is a big science-fiction movie starring a high-budget movie star (*Star Wars*, *Lord of the Rings*, *Avatar*, or *Avengers*)

- Movie 2 is a classic romance comedy starring a popular actor and actress combination who have already done several romance comedies before (*Romancing the Stone*, *Sleepless in Seattle*, or *Groundhog Day*)

- Movie 3 is a big-ticket drama piece starring several former Academy Award winners set in a foreign location (*Out of Africa* or *Titanic*)

- Movie 4 is an art-house period piece movie starring familiar, established actors (*Downton Abbey* or *Little Women*)

Next, we want to construct a simple decision matrix to logically evaluate our movie options based on specific criteria. We will assign scores from 1 to 10, where 1 represents the least desirable and 10 represents the most desirable, to assess each criterion:

Decision Matrix				
Criteria (1 - 10)	Movie 1 Science Fiction	Movie 2 Romantic Comedy	Movie 3 Drama	Move 4 Art House
Acting	4	9	8	10
Directing	4	9	7	8
Storyline	5	7	9	6
Dialog	4	8	9	9
Genre	8	7	6	4
Special Effects	9	4	4	3
Raw Total	34	44	43	40
Raw Score (% of Max)	57%	73%	72%	67%
Unweighted Rank	4	1	2	3

Figure 5.3: Simple decision matrix example

Setting up the decision matrix can take a lot of thought and collaboration between stakeholders. There is significant research, discussion, and debate that is required to establish the decision evaluation criteria. The key steps in the stakeholder collaboration necessary to build a comprehensive and relevant decision matrix are:

1. **Capture your options:** The options being evaluated should be mutually exclusive and collectively exhaustive. Mutually exclusive means that the options do not overlap, and collectively exhaustive means that the options cover all possible alternatives given the universe in which you are operating (in our movie selection example, that would mean only evaluating the movie theaters within driving distance). The decision matrix is designed to ensure that all options are considered and that there is no overlap or gaps in the evaluation.

2. **Determine evaluation criteria:** The next step is to establish the criteria upon which the different options or alternatives will be evaluated. The number of criteria is highly dependent upon the importance of the decision (and the costs associated with being wrong) and the number and diversity of stakeholders. A general rule of thumb is somewhere between 6 to 12 criteria – too few, and it becomes too difficult to differentiate between options; too many and the process can quickly become bogged down. Once you have finalized the criteria, enter them as column headers in the decision matrix.

3. **Determine the criteria rank:** The final step is to rank or rate each of the criteria for our options (or movies, in this example). For each cell of the decision matrix, we will enter a value (usually from 1 to 10) that indicates how well that criteria maps to that particular option (in our case, a movie).

Based on how we have set up our movie criteria evaluation rankings, the highest-ranked movie is the romantic comedy, followed closely by the big-time drama and art house movie. The science-fiction movie was a distant fourth in the rankings.

Pugh decision matrix

A Pugh decision matrix, invented by Stuart Pugh, is a qualitative technique used to rank the multi-dimensional options of an *option set* – the collection of alternatives or choices that are being evaluated and compared against specific criteria. The Pugh decision matrix is a criteria-based decision matrix that uses criteria scoring to determine which potential solutions or alternatives should be selected.

The benefits of using a Pugh decision matrix are:

- **Systematic evaluation:** The matrix provides a structured method to evaluate multiple options and make a decision.

- **Clear criteria**: The criteria used to evaluate the options are explicitly defined, making the decision-making process more transparent.

- **Considers multiple factors**: The matrix allows you to consider various factors such as cost, time, performance, and feasibility when making a decision.

- **Identifies strengths and weaknesses**: The matrix highlights the strengths and weaknesses of each option, making it easier to compare them.

- **Improves communication**: The matrix can be used to communicate and justify the decision-making process to stakeholders.

The difference between the simple decision matrix and the Pugh decision matrix is the addition of the criteria weights as the final *step 4*:

4. **Determine criteria weights**: Not all criteria are of equal value. And this is where the different stakeholders' personal preferences, experiences, and rationale will come into play. Using a scale of 1 to 10 (where 10 is your highest preference) is best in ranking each criterion. Having 6 to 12 criteria helps ensure the process is comprehensive but manageable. Enter the weight for each criterion into the decision matrix.

Let's create a Pugh decision matrix to expand upon our movie-selection processing:

		Pugh Matrix			
Criteria (1 - 10)	Weights	Movie 1 Science Fiction	Movie 2 Romantic Comedy	Movie 3 Drama	Move 4 Art House
Acting	4	9	6	8	3
Directing	6	6	9	7	3
Storyline	9	5	7	9	6
Dialog	4	9	5	5	5
Genre	10	8	7	6	4
Special Effects	9	9	4	4	3
Raw Total		34	44	43	40
Score (% of Max)		57%	73%	72%	67%
Unweighted Rank		4	1	2	3
Weighted Total	420	314	280	257	160
Weighted Score		75%	67%	61%	38%
Weighted Rank		1	2	3	4

Figure 5.4: Pugh matrix

As you can see, when we consider the weighting of the different criteria using the Pugh decision matrix, we get a different outcome (the science-fiction movie being the #1 option) versus the simple decision matrix (where the romantic comedy was the #1 option).

Going through the process of determining criterion weights can be lengthy, especially if your evaluation group is large and diverse. Moreover, getting to a single weight for each criterion can be a challenge. But interactively changing the weights and seeing the results on the outcomes can be eye-opening in understanding which criteria are most valuable and most sensitive to the evaluation process.

In summary, a decision matrix and a Pugh decision matrix compare options or alternatives based on multiple criteria. In *Chapter 6*, we will talk about the role of a Confusion Matrix in evaluating the performance of a classification algorithm in support of our decision matrix.

OODA loop

The OODA loop is a four-cycle **observe–orient–decide–act** process developed by military strategist and United States Air Force Colonel John Boyd. Boyd developed the OODA concept to support aerial combat – dogfights – where real-time decision-making during a dogfight can mean the difference between survival or death.

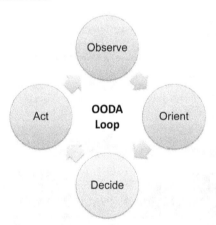

Figure 5.5: OODA decision loop

The OODA loop approach accentuates the critical importance of agility in making informed decisions when operating in a real-world environment. The four stages of OODA are:

- **Observe**: What is the current situation? What are the factors affecting the current situation? What is the rationale driving the need to change the current situation? What are the costs or ramifications of maintaining the current situation?

- **Orient**: Where are you operating currently, given where you want to be or need to go? What is your desired outcome? How far away are you from that desired outcome?

- **Decide**: What actions or decisions do you need to make to reach your desired outcome? What are the benefits of those decisions or actions? What are the potential impediments to your actions? What are the ramifications of decision failure?

- **Act**: What's your action plan given those potential impediments? What's the approach and method that you will take to execute your actions? How will you measure the effectiveness of those decisions? How will you incorporate what you've learned into your next decision?

Yes, embrace your internal Top Gun Maverick!

We have presented three effective decision-making frameworks that are applicable to most situations, depending on the various costs and risks associated with the decision at hand. That's a fabulous start! However, even when utilizing a decision matrix, it is vital to employ critical thinking to verify the reliability and validity of the decision matrix's outcomes.

Critical thinking in decision making

Critical thinking is the rational and objective analysis, exploration, and evaluation of an issue or subject to form a viable and justifiable judgment. However, to truly understand critical thinking, I believe that one must first understand objectivity.

Objectivity, at its core, is the foundation for making intelligent and well-informed decisions. When engaging in the decision-making process, it is crucial to approach the process with an open mind, free from preconceived notions. If you already have a pre-determined decision in mind, you run the risk of selectively seeking data that confirms your position and disregarding information that contradicts your beliefs. Consequently, prioritizing objectivity and consciously avoiding personal biases are essential for mastering critical thinking and thus informed decision-making.

As discussed in *Chapter 1*, organizations with various missions gather your personal data to influence your decisions. Critical thinking is your most potent weapon in a world where half-truths, fake news, and outright lies can be presented as *truth*.

Figure 5.6: Keys to critical thinking

Let's explore the preceding keys to critical thinking in slightly more detail:

- **Don't trust that first answer**. It's very easy (and lazy) to accept the initial answer as "good enough." But *good enough* is usually not good enough and there are typically better answers available with more exploration. One needs to be disciplined in investing the time and effort to explore whether there is a better "good enough" answer.

- **Be skeptical**. Never accept someone's *statement of fact* as truly a *fact*. Question what you read and hear. Accepting what someone says at face value is lazy...and potentially dangerous. Learn to discern facts from opinions. You know what they say about opinions...

- **Consider the source**. When gathering information, consider the credibility, experience, and, most importantly, the agenda of the source. Not all sources are of equal value. The source's credibility is highly dependent upon the biases and prejudices of the source.

- **Don't seek answers you wish to hear**. Don't wait for the answer that you want to hear and ignore what else is being said. Focus on listening for the answers that you didn't expect to hear. That's the moment when learning really starts.

- **Embrace struggling**. The easy answer isn't always the best answer. The easy answer is seldom the best answer given that we are living in an extremely complex and dynamic world.

- **Stay curious**. Nurture an insatiable appetite for learning. This is especially true in today's world where new technologies such as AI and machine learning are evolving so rapidly. Curiosity may have killed the cat, but I wouldn't want a cat making decisions for me anyway.

- **Apply the reasonableness test**. Does what you read make logical sense to you? Is what you are hearing substantially different than what the majority of experts are saying? Would you bet a month's salary on what you heard as being true? While technology is changing rapidly, societal norms and ethics aren't.

- **Pause to think**. Find a quiet place to sit, take a deep breath, and think about everything you've pulled together. Does it make sense? Does it all hang together, or do you have to make significant leaps of faith to make the story work? Take the time to carefully contemplate the ramifications of your action before rushing to the answer.

- **Conflict is good...and necessary.** Life is full of trade-offs, where we are forced to strike a delicate balance between numerous competing factors by increasing one factor while reducing another. Instead of avoiding these conflicts, embrace them. Trying to optimize across conflicting views and perspectives is the fuel that powers innovation.

And finally, here's one from my mom: if it sounds too good to be true, that's probably the case.

Summary

Everything about AI and data literacy can be applied to help us make more rational and informed decisions. Decisions represent the crucial juncture where theory and practical application merge, ultimately benefiting society as a whole. By harnessing the power of AI and understanding how to effectively interpret and utilize data, we empower ourselves and society to make choices that are grounded in reason and knowledge, leading to positive outcomes for all.

And while not every decision will require a formal decision matrix process, you'd be surprised how quickly one can develop informed decision-making as a muscle memory. And in a world where organizations are trying to influence your behaviors, beliefs, and actions through half-truths, white lies, fake news, and alternative facts, informed decision-making is an invaluable skill.

In the next chapter, we will delve into the fundamental statistical concepts that are essential for individuals and society to develop informed decision-making capabilities.

References

1. Sensitivity Analysis: `https://www.investopedia.com/terms/s/sensitivityanalysis.asp`

2. Monte Carlo Technique: `https://www.investopedia.com/terms/m/montecarlosimulation.asp`

3. Toronto Star. *When U.S. air force discovered the flaw of averages*: `https://www.thestar.com/news/insight/2016/01/16/when-us-air-force-discovered-the-flaw-of-averages.html`

4. Harvard Ed Magazine. *Beyond Average* by Todd Ross: `https://www.gse.harvard.edu/news/ed/15/08/beyond-average`

Join our book's Discord space

Join our Discord community to meet like-minded people and learn alongside more than 4000 people at:

`https://packt.link/data`

6

Prediction and Statistics

In the fourth component of the AI and Data Literacy Educational Framework, we focus on prediction and statistics capabilities. Being **prediction- and statistics-savvy** involves leveraging patterns, trends, and relationships uncovered in the organization's vast data troves to make predictions about what is likely to happen to power more accurate, precise decisions.

Probabilities support the predictions that we make as part of our everyday lives. We watch the news for predictions about tomorrow's weather. We use GPS to predict how long driving to the movie theater will take. We read columns from sports experts who provide predictions about whether our favorite sports team will win. And it is from the foundation of statistics that we determine the probabilities that help us predict what is likely to happen.

Having a solid grasp of statistics goes beyond mere theoretical knowledge; it empowers us to make more accurate predictions and, subsequently, better decisions. It serves as the foundation for comprehending essential concepts such as averages, variances, and probabilities. By understanding these fundamental statistical measures, we gain insights into the central tendencies, variabilities, and likelihoods associated with data. However, the true value lies in applying this understanding to our decision-making process.

For example, the complexities surrounding the COVID-19 vaccination scenario provide a poignant illustration of the vital importance of statistics in making informed decisions. Understanding and analyzing vetted scientific data, such as vaccine efficacy rates and the vaccine's real-world impact, is essential in making informed decisions about personal and public health.

This underscores the necessity of being well informed with statistical data and capable of critically evaluating that data to make choices that have a tangible impact on individual lives and the broader society. Survival as a species and success as humans depends upon our ability to improve the odds of making more informed decisions. Understanding statistics and probabilities can help in making those more informed decisions.

To put it concisely, the following topics will be covered in this chapter:

- What is a prediction?
- Understanding the relationship between statistics and probabilities
- Probabilities are still just probabilities, not facts
- Introducing the role of the confusion matrix
- Understanding false positives and false negatives with an example

What is prediction?

A **prediction** is a statement about the likelihood of a future event. Predictions are an intrinsic part of our everyday lives. From weather forecasts to GPS estimations and sports predictions, experts and algorithms analyze historical data and current contextual factors to discern patterns, trends, and relationships, which inform their predictions. By blending insights from the past with present information, these predictions help us plan, make informed decisions, and navigate the world with greater certainty and efficacy.

We know that past performance is highly predictive of future actions and behaviors. Look no further than the infield shift in baseball (since outlawed in 2023), where infielders are positioned on the playing field based on the predictions of that batter's hitting tendencies.

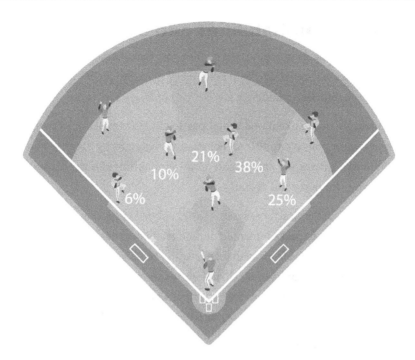

Figure 6.1: Infield shift in baseball based upon batter hitting predictions

And while the **Securities and Exchange Commission (SEC)** cautions investors against assuming that a fund's past performance guarantees future results, it is worth acknowledging that well-managed funds create a predictable track record of consistently outperforming poorly managed funds over time. Past performance provides valuable insights into a fund's management strategies, risk management practices, and overall track record. Astute investors recognize the significance of carefully evaluating a fund's historical performance alongside other pertinent factors, such as the fund's investment philosophy, portfolio composition, and the expertise and experience of its management team, to increase the probability of achieving superior investment outcomes.

This next section will focus on critical fundamental statistical concepts. And while statistics is probably an area of math where many people struggle, we will focus on providing a pragmatic description of these fundamental concepts and their roles in powering more informed decisions.

Understanding probabilities and statistics

Making predictions about likely outcomes is a challenging task. As famously stated by Yogi Berra, *"It's tough to make predictions, especially about the future."* Accurate predictions rely on a nuanced understanding of probabilities, confidence levels, and confidence intervals.

Probability is a measure of the likelihood that a particular event will occur, typically expressed as a percentage (ranging from 0% to 100%). For example, examining Barry Bonds' 2004 season with the San Francisco Giants, we can calculate the probability of him getting a hit as 36.2% (equivalent to 36.2 hits for every 100 at-bats).

Understanding probabilities is vital for assessing the likelihood of specific outcomes, equipping us with the necessary insights to make informed decisions. It is crucial to acknowledge that probabilities serve as estimates derived from available data and statistical analysis. While probabilities provide a framework for evaluating relative likelihoods, it is important to remember that they do not guarantee definitive outcomes. Therefore, to enhance the effectiveness of our predictions, it becomes imperative to harness the power of statistics.

Statistics is the practice or science of collecting and analyzing numerical data in large quantities, especially to infer proportions as a whole from those in a representative sample. By leveraging statistical techniques, we can analyze patterns, identify correlations, and uncover valuable insights that enable us to make more accurate and reliable predictions.

When using statistics to help us calculate probabilities and make predictions, we need to understand the statistical concepts of the mean (or average), variance, standard deviation, confidence intervals, and confidence levels. These are basic statistical concepts that everyone needs to understand in order to leverage statistics to make more informed decisions. Let's define these basic concepts:

- The **mean or average** is the sum of a collection of numbers divided by the count of numbers in the collection.
- **Variance** measures the variability of the numbers or observations from the average or the mean of that same set of numbers or observations. Variance measures how dispersed the data is for the mean.
- **Standard deviation** is simply the square root of the variance. A low standard deviation means data is clustered around the mean, and a high standard deviation indicates data is more spread out. A standard deviation near zero indicates that data points are close to the mean. In contrast, a high or low standard deviation indicates that data points are respectively above or below the mean.

- The **confidence interval** is the range of values you expect your estimate to fall between for a certain percentage of the time if you rerun your experiment or re-sample the population similarly.

- The **confidence level** is the percentage of time you expect to reproduce an estimate between the upper and lower bounds of the confidence interval.

Let's walk through a simple example of the application of the statistical concepts of mean, standard deviation, and confidence level.

A survey of 100 **British (GB)** and 100 **American (USA)** viewers found that both groups watched an average of 35 hours of TV per week[1]. But we can quickly see in the following figure that the viewing patterns between the two parties vary widely.

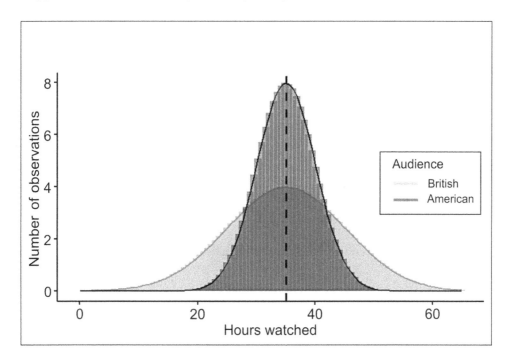

Figure 6.2: Average hours of TV watched

The Brits had a larger variance in the number of hours watched versus the Americans. So, as can be seen in *Figure 6.3*, even though both groups have the same mean (**35**), the Brits had a wider confidence interval than the Americans because of a higher variance in their data. And trying to make predictions without understanding the associated confidence levels can lead to erroneous and even dangerous decisions.

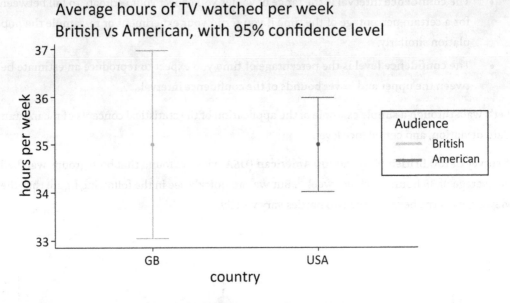

Figure 6.3: Averages + Variances yield confidence levels

Determining confidence levels is critical when trying to make decisions based on probabilities. A confidence level refers to the degree of certainty or likelihood that a particular range of outcomes contains the true population parameter. For example, a 95% confidence level means that if the same estimation procedure were repeated multiple times, 95% of the intervals calculated would contain the true population parameter (two standard deviations from the mean).

 For a normally distributed data set, the values within one standard deviation of the mean account for about 68% of the group, while those within two standard deviations account for about 95%, and those within three standard deviations account for about 99.7%.

The point of this discussion on averages and confidence levels is the following.

When using predictions to make decisions, there are no absolutes. Everything is based on the probability of something happening and the confidence (confidence intervals and confidence levels) of that prediction.

But even with confidence levels, probabilities are still probabilities, and the probability of 99% still means that there is a 1% chance of being wrong. Let's look at a real-world example of how even the best-constructed models cannot avoid the random roll of the dice.

Probabilities are still just probabilities, not facts

FiveThirtyEight.com is one of the most respected analytics sites on the internet. The quality of its predictions is legendary. In the 2008 presidential election of Obama versus McCain, *FiveThirtyEight* (and its founder Nate Silver) correctly predicted the presidential winner in 49 out of 50 states, as well as the winner of all 35 Senate races[2]. As if that was not enough, in the 2012 presidential election of Obama versus Romney, *FiveThirtyEight* correctly predicted not only Barack Obama's victory but also the outcome of the presidential contest in all 50 states.

With that track record as background, *FiveThirtyEight* predicted a 58.5% probability that the Republicans would gain control of the US Senate by taking 51 or more seats in the 2022 midterm elections, as highlighted in the analysis in the following figure:

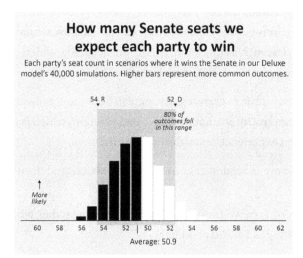

Probabilities of Republicans Winning Senate Seats

Republican Seats	Probability
51	17.7%
52	16.3%
53	12.7%
54	7.7%
55	3.2%
56	0.9%

Probability of Republicans Controlling Senate	58.5%

Figure 6.4: FiveThirtyEight 2022 midterm elections predictions

Unfortunately, even the best and brightest can't always predict the future, and the realities of probabilities caught up with *FiveThirtyEight*. Not only did the Republicans not gain control of the Senate in the 2022 midterm elections (which *FiveThirtyEight* had predicted at a 58.5% probability) but the Democrats even gained a seat (which *FiveThirtyEight* predicted at an 11.7% probability).

While statistics is probably no one's favorite topic (except both my actuarial friends), everyone needs to understand basic statistical concepts to make informed decisions in a world of incomplete and even conflicting information. And fortunately, statistics such as means, probabilities, and confidence levels are around us every day, especially if you are a sports fan or an online gambler (if you want to improve your gambling expected returns, take a primer in statistics).

With a foundation in some basic statistics, it's now time to explore how we can use an important statistical concept – a confusion matrix – to help us make more informed decisions. The confusion matrix helps us assess the effectiveness of a model by providing basic statistical parameters, which allow us to evaluate the effectiveness of the model.

Introducing the confusion matrix

The previous chapter discussed the Decision matrix and Pugh matrix to help us make informed decisions. The next step beyond the Decision matrix and Pugh matrix is the confusion matrix, an aptly named statistical construct.

A confusion matrix is used to evaluate the performance of an AI/ML model by comparing the predicted results with the actual results. The matrix shows the number of true positive, true negative, false positive, and false negative predictions made by the model. In other words, it shows the number of correct and incorrect predictions made by the model. It can be used to calculate a variety of AI/ML model performance metrics, such as precision, recall, and accuracy, which can help to identify the strengths and weaknesses of the AI/ML model.

For example, let's say I'm a shepherd, and my job is to correctly distinguish between *my sheepdog protecting my sheep* and *a wolf out to eat my sheep*. Unfortunately, I have bad eyesight, which is not a good trait for a shepherd. Consequently, I experience many decision errors:

- 10% of the time, I mistake a wolf for my sheepdog, take no protective action, and the wolf causes $2,000 of damage.
- 5% of the time, I mistake my sheepdog for a wolf and accidentally kill the sheepdog, which leaves the flock unprotected, resulting in $5,000 of damage.

So, let's set up a confusion matrix to help me make a more informed decision about whether that unknown animal in the grove is a wolf or a sheepdog. There are four potential outcomes when the shepherd is trying to ascertain whether an animal among the flock is a *sheepdog*, which is there to protect the sheep, or a *wolf*, which is there to prey on the sheep. Two of these four outcomes represent the correct assessment of the situation:

- The true positive is a case of correctly identifying a wolf as a wolf and taking the appropriate protective action.
- The true negative is the case of correctly identifying my sheepdog as a sheepdog and not taking any unnecessary action.

However, the other two outcomes represent an incorrect assessment of the situation:

- The false positive (or the Type I Error) is a result that indicates that a given condition is present when it actually is not present. In our example, a false positive would be incorrectly identifying the animal as a wolf when it is actually my sheepdog (and I accidentally shoot the sheepdog that is protecting the sheep).

- The false negative (or the Type II Error) is a result that indicates that a given condition is not present when it actually is present. In our example, a false negative would be incorrectly identifying the animal as my sheepdog when, in reality, it is a wolf (and I ignore the wolf, and it feasts on the sheep smorgasbord).

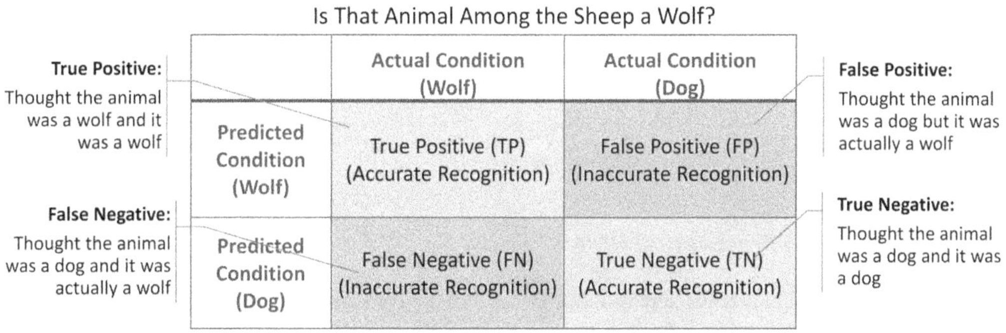

Figure 6.5: Shepherd's decision-making confusion matrix

The confusion matrix allows us to assess the goodness of fit and accuracy of a decision-making model through the following measures.

- Precision = TP / (TP + FP)
- Recall or sensitivity = TP / (TP + FN)
- Specificity = TN / (FP + TN)
- Accuracy = (TP + TN) / (TP + FP + TN + FN)

Now let's say we want to explore building an AI-based Wolf Detection app on my smartphone to help improve my ability to distinguish a wolf from a dog. I need to determine if there is sufficient decision-making improvement from the Wolf Detection app to justify investing in the app.

Remember, before ideating the Wolf Detection app, I (as the shepherd) had the following outcomes:

- False positives 10% of the time, where I mistook a wolf for a sheepdog, took no action, and the wolf caused $2,000 of damage.

- False negatives 5% of the time, where I mistook a sheepdog for a wolf, and accidentally killed the sheepdog, leaving the flock unprotected, which caused $5,000 of damage.

We get the following confusion matrix if we apply these performance numbers across 100 occurrences:

Without AI-Based Wolf Detection App		
	Actual Condition Wolf	Actual Condition Dog
Predicted Condition Wolf	True Positive (75%) = 75 Occurrences No Cost	False Positive (10%) = 10 Occurrences Cost Per Occurrence = $2,000 Total Costs = $20,000
Predicted Condition Dog	False Negative (5%) = 5 Occurrences Cost Per Occurrence = $5,000 Total Cost = $25,000	True Negative (10%) = 10 Occurrences No Cost

Table 5.1: Costs of bad decisions without Wolf Detection apps

Following the previous definitions, the corresponding decision-making metrics without the Wolf Detection app are:

- Precision = 88%
- Recall/sensitivity = 94%
- Specificity = 50%
- Accuracy = 85%

Using the AI-based Wolf Detection app across 100 occurrences, we get the following improvements in false positives and false negatives:

With AI-Based Wolf Detection App		
	Actual Condition Wolf	Actual Condition Dog
Predicted Condition Wolf	True Positive (80%) = 80 Occurrences No Cost	False Positive (4%) = 4 Occurrences Cost Per Occurrence = $2,000 Total Cost = $8,000
Predicted Condition Dog	False Negative (1%) = 1 Occurrence Cost Per Occurrence = $5,000 Total Cost = $5,000	True Negative (15%) = 15 Occurrences No Cost

Table 5.2: Costs of bad decisions with Wolf Detection apps

Decision-making performance metrics using the Wolf Detection app are:

- Precision = 95%
- Recall/sensitivity = 99%
- Specificity = 79%
- Accuracy = 95%

Let's bring this all together into a single table:

	Without Wolf Detection App	With Wolf Detection App	Improvement	% Improvement
Precision	88%	95%	7 points	8.0%
Recall/Sensitivity	94%	99%	5 points	5.3%
Specificity	50%	79%	29 points	58.0%
Accuracy	85%	95%	10 points	11.8%

Table 5.3: Decision-making improvement using the Wolf Detection App

The **Return on Investment (ROI)** then equals:

- Reduction in false positives from 10% to 4% (which saves $2,000 per occurrence)
- Reduction in false negatives from 5% to 1% (which saves $5,000 per occurrence)

Finally, the expected value per prediction:

= ($2,000 * Change in FP%) + ($5,000 * Change in FN%)

= ($2,000*.06) + ($5,000*.04)

= $320 average savings per nightly occurrence ($115,840 annually)

Now I have the criterion for making an informed decision on buying that AI-based Wolf Detection app.

To enhance our analytic model's effectiveness and make more-informed decisions, it is crucial to refine the model by seeking to minimize model false positives and false negatives, thereby reducing model confirmation bias. By actively addressing model false positives and false negatives, we can improve the reliability, accuracy, and effectiveness of our model and the resulting decisions.

False positives, false negatives, and AI model confirmation bias

After explaining the confusion matrix and understanding how it can inform us about our AI model's performance, we must now explore the significance of false positives and false negatives in addressing a critical obstacle faced by AI models: confirmation bias. By understanding the performance metrics associated with false positives and false negatives, we can tackle one of the major challenges associated with AI models head-on.

Confirmation bias is a cognitive bias that occurs when people give more weight to evidence supporting their existing beliefs while downplaying or ignoring evidence contradicting those beliefs.

AI model confirmation bias can occur when the data used to train the model is unrepresentative of the population the model is intended to predict. AI model confirmation bias can lead to inaccurate or unfair decisions and is of significant concern in fields such as employment, college admissions, credit and financing, and criminal justice, where the consequences of incorrect predictions can be severe.

Hiring Applicants

Criminal Sentencing

Financing and Loans

Apartment Rentals

College Admissions

Jury Selection

Figure 6.6: Areas where AI is being used to guide decisions

Mitigating a model's false positives and false negatives plays a vital role in reducing the impact of model confirmation bias and ensuring responsible and effective decision-making. By minimizing false positives, we avoid making incorrect assumptions or taking unnecessary actions based on erroneous predictions. This prevents us from inaccurately predicting outcomes and improves the effectiveness of our decision-making process. On the other hand, reducing false negatives ensures that we don't miss important opportunities due to biases in our model.

By striving to balance and minimize both false positives and false negatives, we create a more accurate and unbiased model. Mitigating false positives and false negatives helps to ensure that the model's predictions are more objective and reliable, enabling us to make more informed decisions based on a more accurate assessment of the data.

Let's look at a real-world situation where the impact of false positives, false negatives, and confirmation bias can have devastating personal and societal impacts.

Real-world use case: AI in the world of job applicants

In 2018, about 67% of hiring managers and recruiters used AI to pre-screen job applicants. By 2020, that percentage had increased to 88%[3].

Poorly constructed and monitored AI models introduce biases into the decision process, lack accountability and transparency, and do not necessarily even guarantee to be effective in hiring the right applicants. These AI hiring models fail by:

- Accepting (hiring) a candidate whose resume and job experience closely match the AI model metrics, behavioral characteristics, and performance assumptions (false positive)
- Rejecting highly qualified candidates whose resumes and job experience don't closely match the metrics, behavioral characteristics, and performance assumptions underpinning the AI models (false negative)

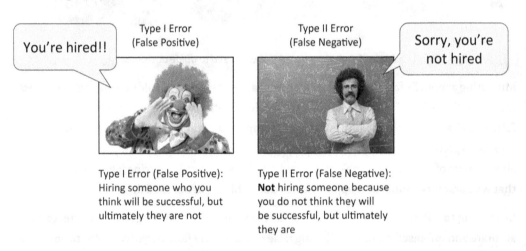

Figure 6.7: AI-based hiring model (Type I and Type II Errors)

The good news is that these problems are solvable.

For the false positive Type I Error, (hiring an applicant the AI model believes will be successful, but in the end, the applicant fails), most HR systems track the performance of every employee, and can easily identify if a hire is not meeting performance expectations. The *bad hire* data can be fed back into the AI training process so that the AI model can learn how to avoid future *bad hires* (or future false positives).

For the false negative Type II Error, (the *missed opportunity* of rejecting an applicant that the model believes will be unsuccessful, but ultimately, that person happens to be successful else-where), the learning process requires more creativity. These false negatives are hard to track but tracking them or the *missed opportunities* is necessary if we want to leverage the false negatives to improve the AI model's effectiveness. And this is where data gathering, instrumentation, and creativity come to bear!

The danger of AI model confirmation bias is that it can feed upon itself if left unchecked, creating an echo chamber effect that targets the same customers and the same activities, thereby contin-uously reinforcing preexisting AI model biases. The long-term ramifications can be disastrous from business viability and regulation liability perspectives.

We can address the dangers of AI model confirmation bias by engineering a feedback loop that continuously learns from the data on false positives and false negatives to retrain and improve the effectiveness of the AI model. The data science team can instrument this feedback loop to measure the effectiveness of the model's predictions so that the AI model can get smarter with each prediction. *Figure 6.8* highlights the key steps in constructing an AI model feedback loop. The feedback loop uses the results from the confusion matrix to tweak the weights used in training the AI model to improve the accuracy and effectiveness of the AI model outcomes.

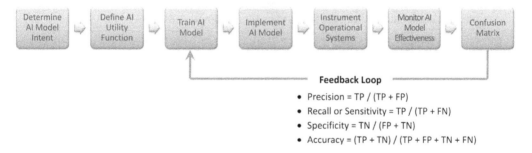

Figure 6.8: Constructing an AI model feedback loop

Instrumenting operational systems to support the preceding AI model feedback loop potentially involves integrating sensors, web tags, audit logging systems, and other data capture capabilities into the operational systems and processes to capture the data, which can be fed back to the AI models to measure and improve their performance.

Constructing an AI model feedback loop is critical if we are to build and operationalize AI models that not only mitigate the effect of false positives and false negatives but also use false positives and false negatives to improve their accuracy and effectiveness.

Summary

As mentioned at the start of this chapter, prediction and statistics are all about how we leverage patterns, trends, and relationships to predict what is likely to happen to make more accurate decisions.

In this chapter, we introduced some fundamental statistical concepts and provided a simple example of those statistical concepts in action. We also discussed the dangers of confirmation bias, and how we can leverage the confusion matrix (such an appropriate name) to construct an AI model feedback loop that leverages the AI model's false positives and false negatives to improve the accuracy and effectiveness of our AI models.

The next chapter delves into the crucial concept of value engineering, exploring how organizations can harness the power of AI and data to generate value. Additionally, we will introduce several valuable tools designed to identify and validate the areas and methods through which an organization can create value. It is important to emphasize that without the ability to generate value for the organization, any AI and data literacy program will fall short of achieving true success.

References

1. Scribbr. Rebecca Bevans, *Understanding Confidence Intervals | Easy Examples & Formulas*: https://www.scribbr.com/statistics/confidence-interval/

2. FiveThirtyEight. Nate Silver, *Today's Polls and Final Election Projection: Obama 349, McCain 189*: https://fivethirtyeight.com/features/todays-polls-and-final-election/

3. SHRM. Dinah Wisenberg Brin, *Employers Embrace Artificial Intelligence for HR*: https://www.shrm.org/ResourcesAndTools/hr-topics/global-hr/Pages/Employers-Embrace-Artificial-Intelligence-for-HR.aspx

Join our book's Discord space

Join our Discord community to meet like-minded people and learn alongside more than 4000 people at:

https://packt.link/data

7

Value Engineering Competency

We are now going to cover the fifth component of the AI and Data Literacy Framework – Value Engineering Competency. **Value Engineering Competency** means understanding how organizations can leverage data (big data) and advanced analytics (AI/ML) to create *value*.

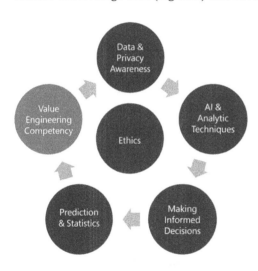

AI possesses the potential to drive systematic improvements across a broad range of industries and business functions. The number of business and operational use cases around which organizations can apply AI to create new sources of *value* is almost unbounded, and that's the problem.

Organizations don't fail because of a lack of use cases; they fail because they have too many.

While many universities and organizations are focused on training more data engineers, data scientists, and ML engineers, we need more folks who can drive organizational alignment and consensus on identifying, validating, valuing, and prioritizing the business and operational use cases that deliver meaningful, relevant, ethical outcomes. We need more business professionals who can translate mathematical (AI/ML) models into economic (value) models. We need more Citizens of Data Science.

To create Citizens of Data Science, we need everyone to understand where and how AI and data can create *value*. And we will frame that value creation understanding via the **Value Engineering Framework** covered later in this chapter.

But before we dive too far into creating value, let's be clear as to what we mean by the word "value." To do that, we must embrace an economics mindset.

Before we begin, here are the topics we'll discuss in this chapter:

- Defining economics and its relationship to value creation
- Introducing the concept of nanoeconomics
- Understanding the Data and AI Analytics Business Model Maturity Index and how to leverage it to become more effective at deriving value from data
- Introducing the role of the Value Engineering Framework to help your organization create new sources of customer, product, service, and operational value
- Getting to know the concept of economies of learning

What is economics? What is value?

Economics is the branch of knowledge concerned with the production, consumption, and transfer of wealth or value. Defining **value**, however, is a tricky proposition. Most organizations have historically relied upon traditional financial measures of value creation, such as:

- Revenue
- Gross profit margin
- Operating profit margin
- **Net Present Value (NPV)**
- **Internal Rate of Return (IRR)**
- **Return On Investment (ROI)**
- **Return On Assets (ROA)**
- Debt-to-equity ratio
- **Earnings Per Share (EPS)**

As discussed in *Chapter 5*, many of these financial measures are lagging indicators; their results depend on the performance of related independent or leading indicators. Organizations must embrace a broader range of measures that define value than just financial measures. If not, these organizations risk creating AI models that result in severe confirmation bias and potentially dangerous unintended consequences.

Organizations that want to embrace AI as an engine of meaningful, relevant, ethical value creation must broaden the measures against which they measure their value creation effectiveness. These broader leading indicators include:

- **Customer satisfaction**: Includes product and service satisfaction, social sentiment, likelihood to recommend (LTR), net promoter score (NPS), product advocacy, and perceived product quality and safety.

- **Employee satisfaction**: Includes employee retention, satisfaction scores, likelihood to recommend, referrals, personal development opportunities, promotion opportunities, creative culture, and support for social programs.

- **Operational execution**: Includes product and operational reliability, predictability, repeatability, stability, safety, agility, and scalability.

- **Partner and ecosystem viability**: Includes partner and supplier financial stability, partner and supplier satisfaction, partner and supplier tenure, business ecosystem or market growth, and partner and supplier Environmental, Social, and Governance (ESG) compliance.

- **Environmental impact**: Includes carbon footprint, waste reduction, recycling, use of recycled materials, greenhouse gas reductions, water conservation, energy efficiency, biodiversity impact, and ESG investing.

- **Societal impacts**: Includes quality of life, access to clean air and clean water, job availability and equality, a minimum living wage, workforce diversity, equity, neighborhood safety, affordable healthcare, affordable housing, affordable education, community engagement, and human rights.

- **Ethical and spiritual impacts**: Includes community outreach and giving-back programs, mentoring opportunities, organizational and community harmony, forgiveness, kindness, tolerance, corporate generosity, compensation, opportunity equality, and ESG. For example, Patagonia's *Worn Wear* program encourages customers to repair and reuse their clothing rather than buy new clothing. The program aims to reduce the environmental impact of textile waste and encourage customers to make more sustainable choices.

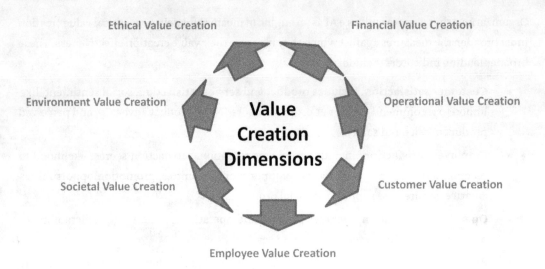

Figure 7.1: Dimensions of value creation

In the context of economics and value creation, it is crucial to consider a broad spectrum of value dimensions beyond financial and operational aspects, encompassing customer, employee, partner, societal, environmental, and ethical dimensions of value definition and realization.

While macroeconomics focuses on the behavior and performance of entire economies, and microeconomics examines individual agents or entities, there is a need to introduce a more detailed level of economic theory to identify and codify the predictable behavioral and performance tendencies of individual entities, whether they are human or devices. This groundbreaking concept is known as nanoeconomics.

What is nanoeconomics?

Nanoeconomics is the economic theory of individual entity (human or device) predicted behavioral and performance propensities. Nanoeconomics is a term I have coined to describe the economic theory of leveraging AI to *uncover* individual human and device predicted behavioral and performance propensities (or analytic insights) that are buried in the organization's customer engagement and operational management data.

From these human-and device-predicted behavioral and performance propensities, organizations can make *precision decisions* to optimize the organization's key business and operational use cases, such as predicting which customers are likely to stop using your products or services, which patients are likely to catch a staph infection, which first-year college students are likely to flunk out, which truck drivers are likely to have a car accident, or which worker is likely to retire.

Propensities encompass a wide range of factors, including tendencies, inclinations, preferences, affinities, passions, associations, relationships, behaviors, tastes, interests, and even biases, all of which contribute to shaping individual actions and decisions. These propensities hold significant potential for organizations, enabling them to deliver more personalized and meaningful experiences that align with individual preferences. However, it is important to recognize that these propensities can also be manipulated or exploited to influence individuals' behaviors and actions in ways that may not align with their best interests or values.

The distinction between propensities and biases can be subtle. For example, I prefer the Chicago Cubs over the Chicago White Sox. When presented with a choice between Cubs or White Sox game tickets or merchandise, I would also always go with the Cubs option (probably with a 99% level of confidence). Smart organizations would leverage this bias or propensity to create a more compelling, differentiated experience and cater to my preferences more effectively.

The key distinction between preferences and biases lies in the presence of discrimination or unfair treatment toward certain protected groups. While preferences are subjective and based on personal choices, biases involve unequal or unjust treatment that denies equal opportunities or rights to individuals solely because of their protected characteristics. It is essential to address biases and discrimination to ensure a fair and inclusive society where everyone has equal opportunities and protections.

Next, we need a value creation roadmap to guide us in identifying and understanding where and how organizations can leverage data and AI to create value. Welcome to the **Data and AI Analytics Business Maturity Index**.

Data and AI Analytics Business Model Maturity Index

The Data and AI Analytics Business Model Maturity Index provides a roadmap for helping organizations become more effective at leveraging data and analytics to power their business and operational models. It provides a benchmark against which organizations can measure their data and analytics progress and effectiveness to understand what good execution looks like from a value creation perspective.

Let's now take time to review the different stages of the Data and AI Analytics Business Model Maturity Index, including the key features and capabilities of each stage, and understand the action plan for navigating the maturity index from retrospective business monitoring to creating a culture of continuous learning and adapting.

Stages

While I was teaching at the University of San Francisco several years ago (where I was an Executive Fellow of their business school), we decided to launch a research project to understand how successful organizations were leveraging data and analytics to enable and differentiate their business models. This research was focused on assessing or measuring the organization's effectiveness at leveraging data and analytics in creating new sources of customer, product, service, and operational value that powered the organization's business models. The following results show you the high-level results of that research:

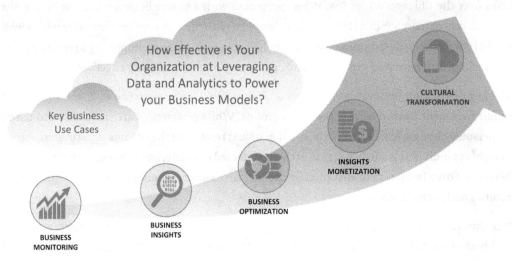

Figure 7.2: Data and AI Analytics Business Model Maturity Index

The Data and AI Analytics Business Model Maturity Index comprises five stages:

1. **Business Monitoring**: This stage encompasses traditional **Business Intelligence (BI)** systems. Organizations collect historical transaction data from their operational systems to create retrospective management reports and operational dashboards that monitor what has happened.

2. **Business Insights**: This stage applies advanced analytics to the organization's data to uncover and codify predicted behavioral and performance propensities (what I'll call analytic insights) for individual humans (customers, patients, doctors, drivers, operators, technicians, engineers, and students) and devices (wind turbines, motors, compressors, chillers, and switches) that predict what's likely to happen next at the individual entity level.

3. **Business Optimization**: This stage applies the customer, product, service, and operational analytic insights uncovered in *Stage 2* to create prescriptive recommendations, or the next best action, to optimize key business and operational use cases.

4. **Insights Monetization**: During this phase, the focus is on the application of customer, product, service, and operational analytic insights to create new sources of value. Many times, these new sources of value come in the form of AI-powered apps (think Uber, Spotify, and Netflix). These revenue streams include entering new markets and audiences, augmenting distribution channels, introducing new products and services, expanding partnerships, and creating a more intuitive, compelling user consumption model.

5. **Cultural Transformation**: This stage seeks to create a culture of continuous learning, adapting, and refining from both machine and human learning perspectives. This stage aims to empower everyone in the organization, democratize ideation, and liberate the unique perspectives, experiences, and strengths of everyone in the organization. As part of Cultural Transformation, organizations need to cultivate both a growth mindset and a tolerance for failure as a means of learning if they want to create a culture that supports curiosity, creativity, innovation, continuous improvement, and, ultimately, success.

As organizations navigate the Data and AI Analytics Business Model Maturity Index, they are going to encounter 3 chasms or inflection points that will threaten their journey. The next section will discuss those 3 inflection points and what the organization needs to do to navigate those inflection points.

Inflection points

Three inflection points in traversing the Data and AI Analytics Business Model Maturity Index inhibit an organization's ability to reach the nirvana of continuous learning and adopting Cultural Transformation (discussed in the previous section). Organizations must adapt new operational, cultural, and economic mindsets to traverse these three inflection points, as shown in the following figure:

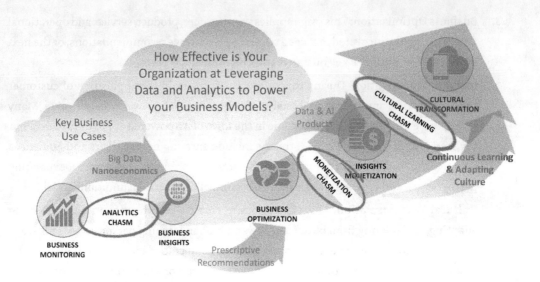

Figure 7.3: Data and AI Analytics Business Model Maturity Inflection Points

The three inflection points and the key to crossing them are:

1. **Analytics Chasm**

   The first inflection point, the Analytics Chasm, requires organizations to transition their use of data and analytics from retrospective BI that monitors what has happened to advanced analytics that predicts what is likely to happen and prescribes recommended actions. The challenge is that crossing the Analytics Chasm is not a technology chasm; it's an economics chasm in how organizations leverage data economic concepts (nanoeconomics) to transition from making decisions based upon averages to making precision decisions based upon an individual entity's predicted behavioral and performance propensities. Crossing the Analytics Chasm also requires crossing the chasm on a case-by-case basis. This requires close collaboration with the business stakeholders to uncover and apply customer, product, service, and operational insights to optimize the organization's key business and operational use cases.

2. **Monetization Chasm**

   The second inflection point transitions from an internal (Stages 2 and 3) to an external focus in Stage 4, Insights Monetization. Stage 4 is about Insights Monetization, not data monetization. Stage 4 is about applying the customer, product, service, and operational insights (or predicted behavioral and performance propensities) uncovered in Stages 2 and 3 to create net new revenue and value creation opportunities. Insights monetization requires business leaders to envision (applying design thinking) where and how the organization can leverage its wealth of customer, product, and operational insights to create AI-infused products and services to enable new markets and audiences, new channels and partnerships, new consumption models, etc.

3. **Cultural Learning Chasm**

   The third inflection point is about fully enabling and empowering the AI-human engagement model to move beyond just optimization to reinvention. Yes, AI models are great at optimizing existing processes, but we need to empower the organization – especially the frontlines of the organization – to reinvent those processes. This requires the transformation of the organizational culture with the capabilities and confidence to empathize, ideate, test, fail, and learn how to reinvent value creation processes, mitigate new operational and compliance risks, and continuously create new revenue opportunities. This means embracing the **economies of learning** – the ability to continuously learn and adapt the organization's AI and human economic assets based on operational interactions.

We now have a roadmap and benchmark against which we can measure our organization's effectiveness at leveraging data and analytics to power our business and operational models. Next, we need a framework to drive cross-organizational collaboration and alignment to identify and prioritize where and how organizations can apply data and AI to create new sources of value.

Value Engineering Framework

One cannot determine the value of one's data in isolation from the business.

The Value Engineering Framework deconstructs an organization's strategic business initiative or business challenge into its supporting business components (including stakeholders, decisions, key performance indicators, and use cases) and data and AI analytics requirements. It starts with understanding how your organization creates value, identifying the internal and external stakeholders involved in that value-creation process, pinpointing the **Key Performance Indicators** (**KPIs**) and metrics against which value-creation effectiveness will be measured, and prioritizing the decisions that the stakeholders need to make to support the organization's value creation processes.

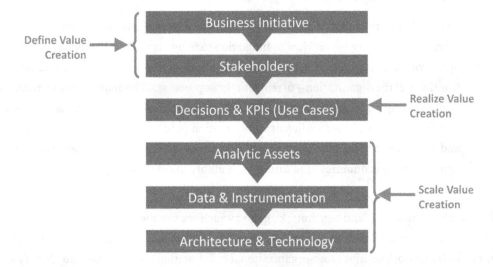

Figure 7.4: Value Engineering Framework

The Value Engineering Framework is a simple process that requires close collaboration across the broad spectrum of internal and external stakeholders who either impact or are impacted by the business initiative. The Value Engineering Framework navigates these three high-level steps:

1. **Define value creation**: First, you must define and understand your organization's value creation processes. That includes understanding the organization's key business initiatives and opportunities, identifying the desired outcomes for these initiatives and opportunities, and brainstorming the KPIs and metrics against which the organization will measure their value creation effectiveness. You also want to collaborate with the organization's key stakeholders – those folks who either impact or are impacted by the value creation process – to understand their desired outcomes, and the KPIs and metrics against which they will measure outcomes' effectiveness. Nail this, and you are at least pointing in the right direction.

2. **Realize value creation**: Next, you must drive collaboration across the different internal and external stakeholders to identify the specific use cases (decisions + desired outcomes + KPIs) that must be optimized to create or realize value. You need to determine for each stakeholder the KPIs and metrics against which they will measure the business initiative's effectiveness.

3. **Scale value creation**: Finally, you need to build the underlying technology, people, process, and cultural foundation that enables the incremental and agile development of the organization's data, analytics, and human capabilities.

Let's now drill into each of the three key steps in the Value Engineering Framework and how to leverage the work and learnings in one step to accelerate and optimize the next step.

Step 1: Defining value creation

The Value Engineering process starts by understanding how the organization creates value (that is, what the organization's business and operational initiatives and objectives are), the KPIs and metrics against which the organization will measure their value creation effectiveness, and the desired outcomes.

One design tool that can help us identify and triage an organization's value creation processes is the Value Definition Design Canvas. The **Value Definition Design Canvas** is a simple tool to drive cross-organizational collaboration and alignment around how the organization defines its value creation processes and the KPIs and metrics against which value creation effectiveness will be measured.

The following figure shows a sample Value Definition Design Canvas completed for Chipotle restaurants' business initiative of *increasing same-store sales*:

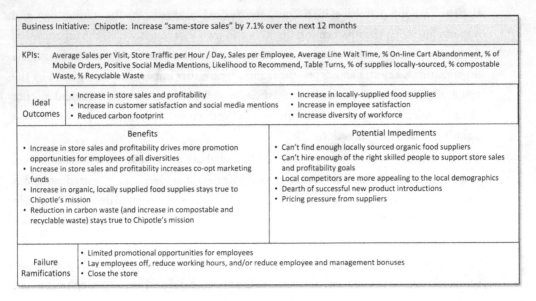

Business Initiative: Chipotle: Increase "same-store sales" by 7.1% over the next 12 months	

KPIs: Average Sales per Visit, Store Traffic per Hour / Day, Sales per Employee, Average Line Wait Time, % On-line Cart Abandonment, % of Mobile Orders, Positive Social Media Mentions, Likelihood to Recommend, Table Turns, % of supplies locally-sourced, % compostable Waste, % Recyclable Waste

Ideal Outcomes	• Increase in store sales and profitability • Increase in customer satisfaction and social media mentions • Reduced carbon footprint	• Increase in locally-supplied food supplies • Increase in employee satisfaction • Increase diversity of workforce

Benefits	Potential Impediments
• Increase in store sales and profitability drives more promotion opportunities for employees of all diversities • Increase in store sales and profitability increases co-opt marketing funds • Increase in organic, locally supplied food supplies stays true to Chipotle's mission • Reduction in carbon waste (and increase in compostable and recyclable waste) stays true to Chipotle's mission	• Can't find enough locally sourced organic food suppliers • Can't hire enough of the right skilled people to support store sales and profitability goals • Local competitors are more appealing to the local demographics • Dearth of successful new product introductions • Pricing pressure from suppliers

Failure Ramifications	• Limited promotional opportunities for employees • Lay employees off, reduce working hours, and/or reduce employee and management bonuses • Close the store

Figure 7.5: Value Definition Design Canvas

The Value Definition Design Canvas is a living document that captures the following information:

- **Business initiative:** This is the business or operational initiative or opportunity the organization is trying to address. For example, improve customer retention or reduce unplanned operational downtime.

- **KPIs:** These are the KPIs and metrics against which the progress and success of the business initiative will be measured. It is vital that we embrace a broad range of value dimensions, including customer, employee, partner, operational, environmental, societal, and ethical.

- **Ideal outcomes:** This articulates the desired outcomes we seek from the successful completion of the targeted business initiative from the perspectives of the different (internal and external) stakeholders.

- **Benefits:** This captures the potential benefits to the successful completion of this initiative from the financial, customer, employee, partner, operational, environmental, societal, and ethical perspectives.

- **Impediments:** This captures the potential obstacles to the successful completion of the targeted initiative, including impediments related to market, competitive, regulatory, technology, data, personnel, skills, financial viability, and cultural factors.

- **Failure ramifications**: This explores the consequences or risks of failure, including potential unintended consequences. This is especially important when you're looking to deploy AI systems.

To monitor the successful execution of the business initiative, it is important to identify the KPIs and metrics for monitoring ideal outcomes, potential impediments, and failure ramifications. Operationalizing these KPIs and metrics is key to identifying and navigating around obstacles, ensuring the project stays on track toward achieving its goals. Without measuring these factors, it becomes challenging to make informed decisions and proactively address concerns as they arise.

Bottom line: if you do not measure for these issues and concerns, then you won't be able to identify and navigate around them.

The following figure shows how we leverage the identification of the KPIs and metrics to monitor and manage the desired outcomes, mitigate potential impediments, and mitigate the ramifications of project failure using the Value Definition Design Canvas:

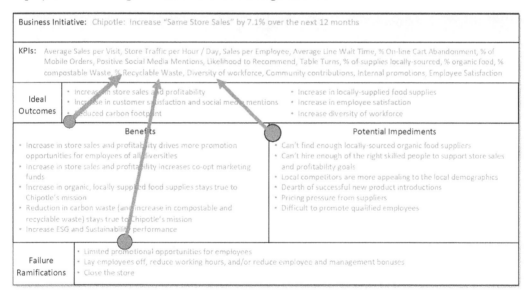

Figure 7.6: KPIs and metrics value validation test

Once the collaborative process has been completed to identify the value-creation processes, the desired outcomes, and the KPIs and metrics for evaluating effectiveness, the next step is to develop an actionable plan to implement and reap the benefits of those efforts. This action plan will center around leveraging business and operational use cases to effectively achieve value creation.

Step 2: Realizing value creation via use cases

A use case is a cluster of interrelated decisions and associated KPIs, supporting a targeted business initiative or business challenge.

The objective of *Step 2* is to embrace a use case-by-use case implementation approach for creating or realizing value. There are multiple benefits of this **use case approach** in driving organizational alignment and consensus on where and how the organization can derive value from the organization's data. The use case approach has the benefits of:

- Establishing value creation – not technology, data, or analytic capabilities – as the linkage between the business and data analytic teams

- Driving organizational alignment in identifying, validating, valuing, and prioritizing the organization's operational use cases

- Supporting a *minimum viable model* approach for delivering meaningful, relevant, responsible, and ethical outcomes while incrementally developing the organization's data and analytic capabilities

- Activating the *economies of learning*, which helps organizations cross the Cultural Learning Chasm highlighted in *Figure 7.3*.

 We will discuss the concept of *economies of learning* later in the chapter.

The heart of a use case is the decisions that the stakeholders are trying to make in support of the targeted value-creation processes or efforts. Decisions are the key linkage point between the business stakeholders and the data and analytics team. While decisions lie at the core of a use case, their relevance stems from the context of the targeted business initiative or challenge they are aimed at addressing. Making relevant, high-value decisions without context is hard (if not nearly impossible).

Decisions are a powerful value enabler because they are:

- **Easily identifiable**: Every business or operational stakeholder knows what decisions they are trying to make because they have been trying to make those decisions for years, if not decades.

- **Actionable**: Unlike a question (a valuable tool for exploration, clarification, and potential feature identification), a decision infers an action.

- **Source of attributable value**: Organizations can determine the quantifiable and attributable value by making improved business and operational decisions. That is, organizations can derive attributable value from making more accurate decisions.

- **Optimizable with data science**: Data science teams specialize in applying analytics to the organization's data to optimize decisions.

- **Collaborative**: Decisions drive collaboration between the business and data science stakeholders to identify the variables and metrics (features) that might be better predictors of performance.

Decisions manifest themselves as the foundation for a use case, while a use case is a business construct for how an organization can create value by addressing a specific operational problem or opportunity. A use case consists of the following elements:

- A KPI that quantifies the desired outcome and tracks the progress and success of the solution.

- A set of key decisions that each stakeholder involved in the solution needs to make, based on relevant data and insights.

- A set of desired outcomes that reflect the expectations and preferences of each stakeholder for achieving the KPI.

Finally, we document the preceding key elements of a use case using the **Use Case Design** template. The following figure drills down into the Chipotle business initiative showing one of the Chipotle use cases – increase store traffic via local events marketing:

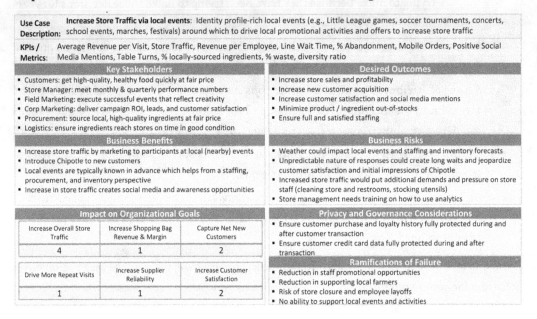

| Use Case Description: | **Increase Store Traffic via local events**: Identity profile-rich local events (e.g., Little League games, soccer tournaments, concerts, school events, marches, festivals) around which to drive local promotional activities and offers to increase store traffic |
| KPIs / Metrics: | Average Revenue per Visit, Store Traffic, Revenue per Employee, Line Wait Time, % Abandonment, Mobile Orders, Positive Social Media Mentions, Table Turns, % locally-sourced ingredients, % waste, diversity ratio |

Key Stakeholders	Desired Outcomes
• Customers: get high-quality, healthy food quickly at fair price • Store Manager: meet monthly & quarterly performance numbers • Field Marketing: execute successful events that reflect creativity • Corp Marketing: deliver campaign ROI, leads, and customer satisfaction • Procurement: source local, high-quality ingredients at fair price • Logistics: ensure ingredients reach stores on time in good condition	• Increase store sales and profitability • Increase new customer acquisition • Increase customer satisfaction and social media mentions • Minimize product / ingredient out-of-stocks • Ensure full and satisfied staffing

Business Benefits	Business Risks
• Increase store traffic by marketing to participants at local (nearby) events • Introduce Chipotle to new customers • Local events are typically known in advance which helps from a staffing, procurement, and inventory perspective • Increase in store traffic creates social media and awareness opportunities	• Weather could impact local events and staffing and inventory forecasts • Unpredictable nature of responses could create long waits and jeopardize customer satisfaction and initial impressions of Chipotle • Increased store traffic would put additional demands and pressure on store staff (cleaning store and restrooms, stocking utensils) • Store management needs training on how to use analytics

Impact on Organizational Goals			Privacy and Governance Considerations
Increase Overall Store Traffic	Increase Shopping Bag Revenue & Margin	Capture Net New Customers	• Ensure customer purchase and loyalty history fully protected during and after customer transaction • Ensure customer credit card data fully protected during and after transaction
4	1	2	

Impact on Organizational Goals (cont.)			Ramifications of Failure
Drive More Repeat Visits	Increase Supplier Reliability	Increase Customer Satisfaction	• Reduction in staff promotional opportunities • Reduction in supporting local farmers • Risk of store closure and employee layoffs • No ability to support local events and activities
1	1	2	

Figure 7.7: Use case design template from Schmarzo's Value Engineering Framework

The preceding template captures the following information for each business and operational use case:

- Use case description and business or operational objectives
- KPIs and metrics against which the progress and success of the use case will be measured
- Use case business benefits
- Use case business risks
- Use case privacy and governance considerations
- Ramifications of use case failure

For our targeted business initiative of increasing same-store sales, we will identify a variety of use cases necessary to support that business initiative.

 If you don't have enough use cases (between 8 to 14), then you have not thoroughly ideated and vetted your targeted business initiative.

To visually depict the interconnections and relationships between these use cases, refer to the following figure. This conceptual mapping showcases the diverse range of use cases that contribute to our overarching goal of increasing same-store sales, enabling a comprehensive understanding of how each use case aligns and synergizes with our business initiative.

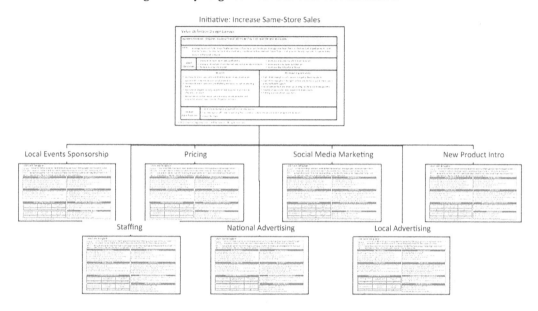

Figure 7.8: Mapping business initiatives to use cases

Now that we have gotten the business and data science teams' alignment around the use cases against which we want to apply data and analytics to create new sources of customer, product, service, and operational value, it's time to focus on building out the underlying data and analytics architecture, and the organization's data and analytic assets.

Step 3: Scale value creation

Scale value creation is a broad and dynamic area because there are always new technologies (such as Generative AI and Large Language Models) and new data concepts (such as data mesh, data fabric, and data lakehouse) that need to be assessed to determine which of these new technologies and concepts are relevant given your situation, experience, and maturity. A deep dive into these topics is the subject of many, many excellent books, so I will not pretend to cover them here.

However, what I will say is this: avoid the "big-bang" approach for building out your scalable data and analytics architecture. Seek an approach that allows you to not only build out your data and analytics capabilities use case by use case but also provides an agile, extensible data and analytics architecture that can also be built out or extended use case by use case.

There are some technology, data, and analytic investments that will need to be built first to start your use case journey, but keep that to a bare minimum (think minimum viable data and analytics environment) and scale as you build out your data and analytics-driven use cases.

The use case implementation approach is the best way to show value to the organization more quickly as the organization builds out its data and analytics capabilities. It builds confidence with the business stakeholders that these efforts are focused on the business, and not just a science experiment. The use case implementation approach is also the best way to activate the **economies of learning**, which is essential for organizations who wish to reach the Cultural Transformation stage (5th level) of Data and AI Analytics Business Model Maturity.

What are the economies of learning?

Organizations are challenged to embrace continuous learning and adapting culture based on the endless march of technological, cultural, and economic innovations. The economies of learning drive this culture of continuous learning and adapting and are how modern organizations learn and adapt more quickly than their competitors.

Economies of learning measure an organization's value creation effectiveness in continuously learning and adapting the organization's human and analytics assets from operational interactions. In a world of digital transformation, the economies of learning – the ability to continuously learn and adapt to this endless march of progressive technology, cultural, and economic innovations – are more powerful than the economies of scale – which seek to protect the retrospective processes and cultures that governed the past.

Creating an economies of learning mindset requires organizations to cultivate a highly iterative, failure-embracing, trying-learning-failing-relearning-retrying economies of learning flywheel that harnesses the natural human creativity in everyone.

Figure 7.9: Economies of learning flywheel

The faster the organization can accelerate its economies of learning flywheel, the faster the company can become in creating new sources of value, driving product and service differentiation, optimizing operational excellence, and growing market share.

Companies best positioned to exploit the economies of learning flywheel exhibit the following characteristics:

- **Compete in knowledge-based markets** where operational, environmental, economic, and social changes and customer and market demands constantly change. That probably describes every industry today.

- **Application of the scientific method to every decision** to facilitate continuous learning – what works, what doesn't, and why – and then adapt the organization's business and operational processes based upon those learnings.

- **Focus on learning, not optimization** because while optimizing yesterday's problems and challenges can yield marginal business and operational improvements, learning and adapting is the only way to survive and learn from tomorrow's problems and challenges.

- **Avoid the "tyranny of precision"** where one refuses to act until the decision is "perfect." Organizations must master incrementally learning to survive and thrive in a dynamic, ever-changing world.

- **Encourage a culture of learning from failures.** Failures are only failures if 1) one doesn't thoroughly consider the ramifications of failure before acting and 2) the lessons from the failure aren't captured and shared across the organization. If you aren't failing and sharing, then you aren't learning.

The use case approach exploits the economies of learning, such that the learnings from one use case can be reapplied to other use cases. Any improvements in the completeness of the data and accuracy of the analytics can ripple through each use case. This is a topic that I covered very thoroughly in my book *The Economics of Data, Analytics, and Digital Transformation*.

This last section of the chapter is going to summarize how organizations can leverage data and analytics to drive value creation or monetization. But it's not data monetization upon which organizations should focus.

Monetize analytic "insights," not data

The term *data monetization* is confusing for many organizations because they believe the best way to derive value from their data is by selling it.

But, the most profitable companies in the world today don't monetize their data by selling it. Leading companies like Apple, Google, Amazon, and Google didn't become the richest companies in the world by selling their data. Instead, these leading digital organizations monetize their data by identifying and packaging the customer, product, service, and operational insights buried in their data to create new sources of value.

Harnessing the Economic Power of Data

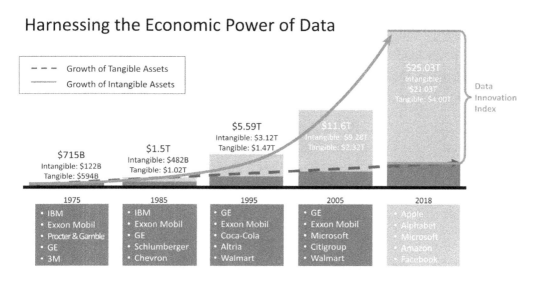

Figure 7.10: Market cap of the most profitable companies

Most organizations should instead be focused on **insights monetization**, which is about leveraging the customer, product, and operational insights (individualized predicted behavioral and performance propensities) buried in your data to optimize key business and operational processes, mitigate risks, create new revenue opportunities, and construct a more compelling, differentiated customer experience.

The data economics concept of nanoeconomics discussed earlier in this chapter is the key enabler of insights monetization. Nanoeconomics leverages AI to *uncover* and quantify individual human and device predicted behavioral and performance propensities (or analytic insights) as **analytic scores**. Analytic scores predict the likelihood of a behavior or action expressed as a single number, such as a credit score, to predict one's likelihood of repaying a loan. These analytic scores are captured in **analytic profiles** that can be applied and reused to optimize the outcomes from the organization's key business and operational use cases.

Analytic profiles are a key-value ore that facilitate the capture, sharing, reuse, and continuous refinement of the individual entities' analytic scores (e.g., credit scores, quality scores, loyalty scores, and health wellness scores). These individual entities can be either *humans* (e.g., customers, patients, doctors, students, teachers, athletes, engineers, or operators) or *devices* (e.g., compressors, chillers, tractors, vacuums, presses, cars, trains, or airplanes).

Analytic Profiles: Codifying and Sharing Asset Predicted Propensities

Analytic Profiles codify, share, reuse, and continuously refine the predicted behavioral and performance propensities (**Analytic Scores**) for the organization's key human and device assets

Patient Care Data	Schmarzo Patient Healthcare Profile	NCE Score	Variance	Trend	External Patient Data
• Demographic	Health Score	92	1.89	⬆	• Diet History (DietPlanner, MyFitnessPal)
• Behavioral Demographics	Wellness Score	92	1.85	↔	
	Diet Score	67	3.25	↔	• Physical Exercise History (Apple Watch, FitBit)
• Psychographics	Exercise Score	82	2.25	⬆	
• Patient care / treatment history	Stress Score	65	1.90	⬇	• Mental Acuity History (Lumosity, CogniFit)
• Patient vital stats history	COVID-19 At-Risk Score	22	2.35	⬇	• Stress History (Stress Doctor, Happify)
	Cancer At-Risk Score	14	1.74	⬆	
• Physician / Nurse care notes	Pulmonary At-Risk Score	02	1.15	↔	• Emotional History (Text, Social)
	Oncology At-Risk Score	08	1.20	⬇	
• Patient comments	Heart Attack At-Risk Score	09	1.25	↔	• Vices History
• Pharmacy/Prescriptions	Stroke At-Risk Score	06	1.10	↔	• Vacation / Relaxation History
• Others...	....				• Others...

Figure 7.11: Role of analytic profiles to capture entity analytic insights

Finally, analytic profiles and analytic scores can be applied to optimize the outcomes from the organization's key business and operational use cases, as shown in the following figure:

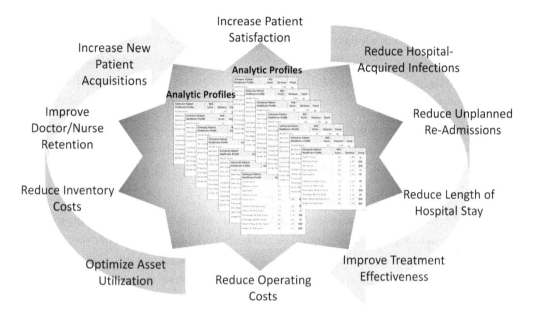

Figure 7.12: Value realization in applying nanoeconomics and analytic profiles to optimize use cases

So, to refresh, we introduced and deep-dived into the 3 phases of the Value Engineering Framework:

- **Step 1**: Define how the organization creates value and measures that value creation effectiveness.

- **Step 2**: Align the organization on an action plan to realize value creation on a use case-by-use case basis.

- **Step 3**: Build a flexible and extensible architecture and organizational structure to scale those value-creation use cases.

There is nothing stopping us now from helping organizations to become more effective at leveraging data and analytics to power their business models.

Summary

Indeed, I said this would be a long chapter, and it was. This chapter represents the culmination of how organizations will ultimately measure the effectiveness of their AI and data literacy programs. In the end, driving *value* is why all organizations – large corporations, small businesses, non-profit organizations, educational and healthcare institutions, and government agencies – exist.

We covered much ground about how organizations leverage their data to create value. And that data-driven value creation conversation starts by understanding how the organization defines *value* and identifying the KPIs and metrics against which these organizations measure their value creation effectiveness.

Once the organization understands how it defines and measures value creation, we move on to the concepts of nanoeconomics, analytic profiles, and business and operational use cases to realize or create value for the organization. The process is straightforward and pragmatic: if you don't first define how your organization defines and measures value creation, it's nearly impossible to create value.

In the next chapter, we are going to discuss and explore the difficult concept of ethics. The challenge of ethics, from an AI and data literacy perspective, is if we can't measure it, then we can't monitor it, manage it, or improve it. This chapter will describe some bleeding-edge ideas on how organizations and society can leverage economic concepts to measure ethics and ensure that AI is working for humans versus humans working for AI.

Join our book's Discord space

Join our Discord community to meet like-minded people and learn alongside more than 4000 people at:

https://packt.link/data

8

Ethics of AI Adoption

Ethics is understanding and applying the moral principles of right and wrong that govern a person's behavior or actions.

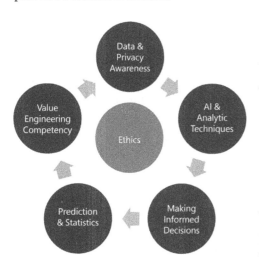

Because so much of what we are doing with AI is mathematics-based and technologically exciting, we sometimes tend to forget the bigger mission of AI – to deliver meaningful, relevant, responsible, and ethical outcomes. Ethics needs to underpin the design, development, and deployment of all AI models, which means everyone needs to understand what is necessary to embed responsible and ethical choices into our AI models.

To prepare Citizens of Data Science for those all-important ethical conversations and design decisions, we'll discuss the following topics in this chapter:

- A foundational understanding of what ethics is
- Exploring the relationship between economics and ethics
- Leveraging the Ethical AI Pyramid to guide the maturation of our AI capabilities
- Understanding the unintended consequences of AI and how to deal with them

Understanding ethics

Ethics are the moral principles governing a person's behavior or actions, the principles of *right and wrong* generally accepted by an individual or a social group. Or as my mom used to say, "Ethics is what you do when no one is watching."

AI ethics, on the other hand, is a field of study that focuses on AI's ethical development, application, and management. AI ethics involves identifying and exploring the potential unintended consequences of AI and considering how AI can be used fairly and responsibly to benefit society.

Ethics is proactive, not passive

Ethics is fundamentally proactive rather than passive. It demands taking appropriate actions in alignment with society's moral standards, instead of merely delegating such responsibility to others. Understanding the distinction between passive and proactive ethics is crucial, and one can find a valuable lesson in the timeless Parable of the Good Samaritan from the Bible.

The Parable of the Good Samaritan recounts the story of a Jewish traveler who is robbed, beaten, and left for dead on the side of the road. While in his beaten state, a priest and a Levite, both respected figures, come across the injured man but choose to pass by on the other side, disregarding his plight. However, a Samaritan, despite the historical enmity between Samaritans and Jews, shows compassion. He tends to the wounded man's injuries, brings him to an inn on his own animal, and ensures his well-being by covering the expenses for his care and accommodation. This parable emphasizes the importance of proactive compassion and crossing societal boundaries to help those in need, irrespective of differences or prejudices.

The priest and the Levite exemplified the passive ethics principle of "do no harm." Technically, they did not do anything wrong by avoiding the injured man. However, that mindset falls short in a world shaped by AI models. It is imperative that our AI models embody proactive ethics, where both the AI models themselves and the AI utility function guiding their operations actively strive to "do good." We must embrace the responsibility to design AI systems that actively seek to benefit and contribute to the betterment of society.

Redefining ethics in the age of AI

AI will force us to reevaluate how we define and measure ethical conduct within our society and our institutions. It is crucial that we prioritize long-term societal benefits over short-term individual gain. Given AI's incredible capacity to learn and adapt at an unprecedented scale, it is imperative that we accurately define, develop, and implement ethical standards in the design, development, and deployment of our AI models. The consequences of getting this wrong could be dire.

But here's the challenge when it comes to discussing AI ethics – if we can't measure it, we can't monitor it, judge it, or improve it. We must, therefore, find transparent ways to measure and instrument ethics, especially as AI becomes more integrated into our daily lives and society at large.

And if we thought that this was a problem that we could get to later, well, SURPRISE! The time to act is *now*. Growing concerns about the potential dangers of ChatGPT, an AI-infused chatbot that uses machine learning techniques to understand natural language and generate human-like responses to user input, have increased the sense of urgency and the dire predictions of the impact of untethered generative AI capabilities:

> *"Whereas the printing press caused a profusion of modern human thought, the new technology achieves its distillation and elaboration. In the process, it [ChatGPT] creates a gap between human knowledge and human understanding."*
>
> — *Henry Kissinger, Eric Schmidt, and Daniel Huttenlocher, Wall Street Journal, February 24, 2023*

> *"Powerful AI systems should be developed only once we are confident that their effects will be positive and their risks will be manageable."*
>
> — *The Future of Life Institute, whose membership includes Elon Musk and Steve Wozniak, on March 29, 2023*

Don't expect Asimov's Three Laws of Robotics to protect us:

- **Law #1**: A robot (AI) may not injure a human being or, through inaction, allow a human being to come to harm.
- **Law #2**: A robot (AI) must obey the orders given to it by human beings except where such orders would conflict with the First Law.
- **Law #3**: A robot (AI) must protect its existence as long as such protection does not conflict with the First or Second Law.

 The Three Laws of Robotics (often shortened to Asimov's Laws) are a set of rules devised by science fiction author Isaac Asimov. The rules were introduced in his 1942 short story *Runaround*.

Unfortunately, these existing three laws of robotics are inadequate when it comes to providing comprehensive guidance for AI models that influence crucial societal decisions in areas such as employment, credit, finance, housing, healthcare, education, taxes, law enforcement, legal representation, social media, content distribution, and more. Codifying ethics is *the* major challenge in steering AI models toward making responsible and ethical choices, ensuring desirable outcomes.

As we discussed in *Chapter 5*, codifying ethics is essential because AI models will continuously learn and adapt – at speeds unfathomable by humans – to maximize *rewards* and minimize *penalties* based on the variables and metrics that comprise the AI model's AI utility function.

But there is good news here, and lots of it. We need to adopt a framework using which we can drive the necessary conversations to ensure that we design, develop, and deploy AI models that deliver meaningful, relevant, responsible, and ethical outcomes. And that framework has been around for a while: economics. Let's dive into the all-important intersection of ethics, economics, and societal well-being.

The intersection of ethics, economics, and societal well-being

It may seem weird to be talking about ethics, economics, and societal well-being in the same conversation. Economics is the discipline of creating and distributing wealth or value. But creating and distributing *sustainable* value must include ethics and societal well-being considerations because without those two components, what sort of value are you really creating?

Ethical behaviors make for good economics

Society can achieve positive economic outcomes driven by the ethics of fairness, equality, justice, and generosity. The Bible, as well as other religious doctrines, is full of ethical lessons that are economic lessons based upon a more holistic definition of *value*. Yes, the Bible is a masterpiece of economics lessons on how society can deliver more relevant, meaningful, responsible, and ethical outcomes.

Economics is defined as a framework for the creation and distribution of wealth or value. Let's illustrate this with an example.

A study conducted in Massachusetts highlights the potential value of a fairness program known as *School Meals for All*[1]. The state currently allocates $2.4 billion each year to address student mental health issues, diabetes, obesity, and cognitive development challenges.

By implementing the *School Meals for All* initiative, the annual cost amounts to $100-120 million, yielding a substantial return on investment of 10 times in the form of enhanced health and education outcomes, all while positively contributing to the well-being of society and its citizens.

In another example, the research conducted by the National Forum on Early Childhood Policy and Programs revealed that investments in early childhood programs can generate a return of $4 to $9 for every $1 invested. Similarly, a 2009 study on the Perry Preschool program, targeting children aged 3 to 5, estimated a return of $7 to $12 per $1 invested[2].

This illustrates that ethical behaviors are just good economics.

One area where people and organizations get confused is understanding the difference between financial measures (which tend to have a short horizon) and economic measures (which tend to have a longer horizon). A quick review of the differences between simple financial metrics and the more encompassing economic measures is critical if we are to define and design AI models that deliver meaningful, relevant, responsible, and ethical outcomes.

The difference between financial and economic metrics

Suppose we use economics to create a framework to define and measure ethical behaviors and decisions. In that case, we must understand the differences between financial and economic metrics.

- **Financial metrics** are used to evaluate the financial performance of an organization. They are typically focused on an organization's short-term financial performance at a given time. Examples of financial metrics include the profit margin, **Return On Assets (ROA)**, **Return On Equity (ROE)**, **Return On Invested Capital (ROIC)**, **Return On Capital Employed (ROCE)**, **Earnings Per Share (EPS)**, **Return On Investment (ROI)**, and debt-to-equity ratio.

- **Economic metrics** are used to evaluate society's overall health and holistic well-being. Economic metrics measure and track the economy's or society's long-term health to help policymakers make more informed economic policy decisions. Examples of economic metrics include **Gross Domestic Product (GDP)**, unemployment rate, **Consumer Price Index (CPI)**, **Producer Price Index (PPI)**, poverty rates, housing starts, and interest rates. These economic metrics focus on a broader range of societal characteristics, including education, healthcare, justice, safety, diversity, society, environment, and citizen well-being.

Understanding the differences in the time horizon (short-term versus long-term) between financial and economic metrics is essential. For example, today, we see individuals and organizations "game" financial metrics by taking actions that have short-term financial benefits to them personally but have high long-term costs to society.

Some recent examples include Bernie Madoff's Ponzi Scheme[3], the Elizabeth Holmes and Theranos scandal[4], the Purdue Pharma opioid epidemic[5], and the FTX crypto facade[6].

However, the more deadly dangers are less obvious. The more toxic dangers are the unfounded conspiracy theories that distract from the proactive ethics necessary to *do good* in addressing critical perils such as climate change, marriage rights, women's rights, public education, income disparity, public healthcare, judicial fairness, and prison reform.

The role of laws and regulations on ethics

One way society dissuades short-term gaming and encourages long-term focus is through laws and regulations. Properly constructed laws and regulations can introduce economic incentives and financial and criminal penalties to spur compliance and adherence. Laws and regulations can change behaviors by changing associated rewards and penalties, such as how cigarette taxes make cigarette smoking less desirable.

In another example, container deposit laws have had a huge impact on beverage container recycling. States with beverage container recycling laws saw a recycling rate of around 60%, while states without beverage container recycling laws reached only about 24%[7].

Expanding the variety of economic measures provides an opportunity to develop laws and regulations that foster ethical behaviors and deter unethical conduct. It is also crucial to carefully approach the construction of these laws and regulations to avoid potentially harmful unintended consequences. By implementing a comprehensive approach, we can strike a balance that incentivizes responsible actions and discourages harmful practices, ensuring that our ethical goals align with tangible outcomes in a manner that avoids unforeseen negative outcomes.

Achieving a responsible and ethical AI implementation

Now that we have laid out the importance of identifying, validating, and integrating metrics that monitor the ethical behaviors of our AI models, let's talk about the implementation challenges in achieving responsible and ethical implementation and execution.

This section of the chapter is going to define the Ethical AI Pyramid and how one can use it to design, develop, and deploy AI models that deliver meaningful, relevant, responsible, and ethical outcomes. We will then transition the Ethical AI Pyramid discussion into a deep dive into the importance of AI model transparency.

The Ethical AI Pyramid

The Ethical AI Pyramid serves as a comprehensive guide for developing AI models that prioritize transparency, impartiality, and continuous learning while aligning with societal laws and norms. By adhering to the principles of ethical AI, this pyramid aims to guarantee the ethical, transparent, and accountable design, development, and management of AI models. It emphasizes the fulfillment of user expectations, organizational values, and compliance with relevant legal and societal standards.

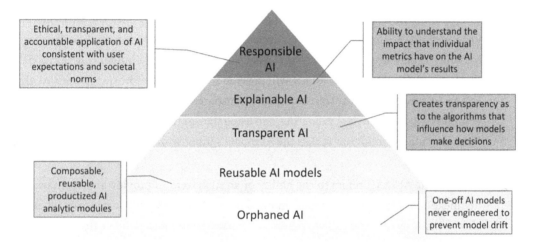

Figure 8.1: Ethical AI Pyramid

As shown in the preceding figure, the Ethical AI Pyramid consists of the following leverages of ethical AI maturity:

- **Orphaned analytics** are one-off AI/ML models developed for a specific operational purpose but were never *productized* to manage ML model drift. ML model drift occurs when an ML model's performance degrades over time as the operating environment for which it was initially developed changes. Over time, orphaned analytics transition from corporate assets that deliver a continuous stream of value to corporate liability in terms of the potentially dangerous and wrong decisions that can be driven by these models.

- **Reusable AI models** are engineered to be shareable, reusable, and extensible economic assets. Reusable AI models manage model drift and are instrumented such that the AI model can learn from the AI model's false positives and false negatives. And while instrumenting for the AI model's false positives and false negatives can require significant work, the ability of the model to learn from its mistakes can also help address AI confirmation bias.

Transitioning from orphaned analytics to reusable AI modules requires organizations to develop a centralized approach for sanctioning and managing the AI modules that get built. The AI modules most likely will be identified and developed in a decentralized environment, but those AI modules must adhere to centrally defined development standards. This transition puts the organization on the path to creating AI assets that appreciate in value the more that they are used – the heart of the economics of data and analytics that I discuss in my book *The Economics of Data, Analytics, and Digital Transformation* (not a bad companion book to grab and read after this book).

- **Transparent AI** uses AI algorithms that provide transparency into the variables and weights the AI model uses to make its decisions. A transparent AI system uses algorithms for which experienced data scientists can determine the variables influencing the model's decisions and recommendations. I will provide some examples of transparent AI algorithms later in this chapter. Transitioning to transparent AI requires an organization-wide commitment to identifying, validating, and using transparent AI algorithms (and avoiding black-box algorithms) that makes the AI model's inner workings visible to experienced data scientists.

- **Explainable AI (XAI)** refers to the ability of an AI system to provide an explanation or justification for its decisions or recommendations. XAI is essential in contexts where decisions made by AI systems have significant consequences, such as in healthcare, finance, and criminal justice. I will talk more about XAI later in this chapter. Transitioning to XAI takes an organizational commitment to make the variables that are used to power the AI model's decisions (the AI utility function) available to everyone who might be impacted by that model. That means communicating those variables in legible terms such as *Customer Age* and not *cust_bdate_yr_mo_day*.

While transparent AI and XAI are related, they address different aspects of an AI system's behavior. A transparent AI system may provide access to its inner workings, which may be challenging to non-experts. An XAI system, on the other hand, may provide understandable explanations for its decisions, but those explanations may not be easily accessible or auditable by stakeholders. To ensure responsible AI, transparency and explainability are essential, and organizations developing AI systems should strive to achieve both.

- **Responsible AI** is a cultural manifestation designed to address various ethical and social issues related to AI's responsible and ethical use, including bias and discrimination, data privacy, transparency and explainability, accountability, and societal impact. The goal of responsible AI is to ensure that AI is developed and used in a way that is transparent, fair, and accountable and respects an individual's privacy and dignity. Transitioning to responsible AI builds upon the earlier levels by adding feedback and audit systems to measure and monitor the AI model's false positives and false negatives, mitigate AI model confirmation bias, and install safeguards to flag and avoid potentially dangerous unintended consequences.

Responsible AI ensures the ethical, transparent, and accountable use of AI technologies consistent with user expectations, organizational values, and societal laws and norms[8].

Ensuring transparent AI

A crucial part of the Ethical AI Pyramid is providing transparency into the variables and metrics – and their associated weights – that the AI models use to make their decisions and recommendations. Several analytic algorithms can be used that provide transparency into the influence that individual variables have on a given decision or recommendation, including:

- **Linear regression** is a widely used statistical technique to model the relationship between a dependent variable and one or more independent variables. Linear regression can be used to identify the influence of individual variables on the dependent variable by estimating the coefficients for each variable.

- **Decision trees** are machine learning algorithms identifying the essential variables influencing a given outcome. Decision trees work by dividing the data into smaller and smaller subsets based on the variables' values, then using these subsets to make predictions about the outcome.

- **Random forests** are machine learning algorithms based on decision trees. They work by building many decision trees and then combining the predictions made by each tree to make a final prediction. Random forests are often used to identify the most critical variables that influence a given outcome.

- **Gradient boosting** is a machine learning algorithm used to build predictive models by sequentially adding simple models, each of which tries to correct the errors made by the previous models. Gradient boosting can be used to identify the most critical variables that influence a given outcome.

- **Lasso and ridge regression** are regularized linear regression types identifying the most critical variables influencing a given outcome. Both techniques work by adding a penalty term to the objective function that is being minimized. This encourages the model to choose fewer variables and reduces the influence of less essential variables.

- **Principal Component Analysis (PCA)** is a dimensionality reduction technique that can be used to identify patterns in data and identify the underlying structure of the data. It can help ascertain the influence of individual variables in a dataset, but it is crucial to understand the limitations and potential biases of this method.

- **Shapley Additive exPlanations (SHAP)** is another technique for addressing the AI transparency challenge[9]. SHAP assigns each feature in the model a value representing that feature's relative importance in driving the predictive model's outcome. SHAP estimates the feature's relative importance by seeing how well the model performs with and without that feature for every combination of features.

Hopefully, the Ethical AI Pyramid can be your guide for the AI implementation lifecycle – defining, developing, and managing – providing the transparency, impartiality, and continuous learning and adaptation necessary for your AI models to align with and reinforce societal laws and norms.

Now that we understand the different levels for delivering ethical AI outcomes, what can we do to brainstorm the potential unintended consequences resulting from the application of AI models?

Understanding unintended consequences

Unintended consequences are unforeseen or unintended results that can result from an action or decision. Unintended consequences can occur when insufficient consideration is given to the second- and third-order potential outcomes of even the best-intended initiatives and decisions. That is, have we given sufficient time and effort to understanding and mapping not only the consequences of our decisions and actions but also understanding and mapping the consequences of those consequences, and even the consequences of those consequences?

There are many examples of *good intentions gone wrong* that yielded devastating unintended consequences, such as:

- The SS Eastland, an ill-designed and unwieldy vessel, was meant to enhance its safety by incorporating additional lifeboats. Ironically, the weight of these lifeboats led to the ship capsizing, resulting in the entrapment and tragic loss of 800 passengers beneath its decks.

- The Treaty of Versailles was intended to establish the surrender terms for Germany, marking the conclusion of World War I. Regrettably, these terms had unintended consequences as they inadvertently bolstered Adolf Hitler and his supporters, ultimately contributing to the outbreak of World War II.

- The Smokey Bear Wildfire Prevention campaign has had a remarkable track record in fire prevention spanning several decades. However, it is now evident that this well-intentioned effort has disrupted the natural fire processes that are crucial for the overall health of the forest. As a result, devastating mega-fires have emerged, consuming everything in their path, including ancient pine trees that withstood the test of time under normal fire conditions for thousands of years.

In the next two sections, let's understand how we can identify and subsequently mitigate the potential negative impacts of unintended consequences.

Identifying unintended consequences

Identifying the potential unintended consequences that might emerge from our actions and decisions is a daunting task. Unable or unwilling to contemplate far-reaching effects, we struggle to grasp the second- and third-order ramifications. Each choice we make has the potential to set in motion a chain of events that extend far beyond our immediate understanding, shaping the ramifications of our actions and decisions in unforeseen ways. To address this challenge, we must embrace a mindset that extends beyond short-term benefits so that we can begin to fathom the complexities of cause and effect.

The **Unintended Consequences Assessment Worksheet** is designed to drive group collaboration in identifying the potential unintended consequences resulting from the application of AI, and then brainstorming the potential economic ramifications of those unintended consequences.

This Unintended Consequences Assessment Worksheet shown in the following figure is a powerful extension to the well-documented and tested Thinking Like a Data Scientist methodology, including the design canvases already associated with the method. And as we learned with the design canvases in the Thinking Like a Data Scientist methodology, it will evolve as we use it and learn what works and doesn't.

Initiative: Launch "Head Start" program to feed all K-6 students at the start of each school day. Desired outcomes: healthier students, improved classroom performance, less classroom disruptions. Key stakeholders: students, parents/guardians, teachers, administrators, community leaders. KPIs: class attendance, grades, graduation rates, crime rate		
Scenario 001: Initiative insults or offends targeted constituents sowing community distrust and political grandstanding		

Value Dimensions	Scenario Factors	Short-term Measures	Long-Term Measures
Financial Impact	•Costs greatly exceed budget and doom additional funding •Political leaders demand a reallocation of funding •Negatively affects budget allocations for similar initiatives •Less budget allocated for initiative than originally budgeted	Program costs vs plan, budget shortfall %, budget over-runs, shrinkage, fraud	% Fraud, % Shrinkage, Food prices, labor costs vs plan
Operational Impact	•Too difficult and costly to find workers to run the program •The quality of meals is substandard •Supply chain and procurement glitches hinder program	Number of meals served, Nutritional quality of meals	Nutritional quality of meals
Stakeholder Impact	•Students do not participate •Students & families highly dissatisfied with the program and take to social media and contact local media •Targeted families question the sincerity of the program	Student participation, Student satisfaction, Administrator satisfaction, Student in-class attendance, Student in-class performance	Student graduation rate, student national testing rank, Students going to college or vocational schools
Societal Impact	•No family or community realized benefits •Negative consequences on in-school performance & behaviors	School attendance rates, Drop out rates, Graduation rates, Classroom performance	Local crime rates, local poverty rates, local property values, Teacher retention, Community satisfaction
Environmental Impact	•Significant waste and discards pollute surrounding areas •Carbon footprint skyrockets from unnecessary transportation of unneeded food	% food wasted, % waste recycled, % recycled materials	% food locally-sourced, % organic food, reduce carbon footprint
Ethical Impact	•Target constituents feel exploited by the media and politicians •Similar programs for more privileged students are exposed		

Figure 8.2: Unintended Consequences Assessment Worksheet

This Unintended Consequences Assessment Worksheet assists in identifying and comprehending the possible unforeseen outcomes of implementing AI within the context of a business-specific initiative. The template records the following vital details:

- **Initiative**: A description of the business or operational initiative against which one plans to apply AI.

- **Scenario**: Identify/brainstorm a potential scenario or unintended consequence that might arise from the execution of that AI-based initiative.

- **Outcomes**: For that scenario, identify the potential outcomes across the financial, operational, stakeholder (customer, employee, or partner), societal, environmental, and ethical dimensions.

- **Variables and metrics**: Then, for each outcome, identify the short-term and long-term variables and metrics that we might want to use to monitor and manage each scenario outcome.

Since several variables will be identified during this exercise, it would be helpful to weigh the relative importance of each of the variables as either high/medium/low or on a scale of 1 to 5.

Mitigating unintended consequences

There are several actions that organizations can take to mitigate the potential impacts of those unintended consequences, including:

1. **Create a formal process.** Then, train everyone on that process to help the organization envision the potential consequences of the decision *before* the decision is made. This should be a multi-disciplinary, collaborative envisioning and exploration process where all ideas from all stakeholders are worthy of consideration.

2. **Engage a broad range of stakeholders.** Bring together a diverse group of stakeholders and constituents who bring different perspectives and experiences to the potential unintended consequences brainstorming process. Those stakeholders and constituents should include internal and external parties with a vested interest in doing the right thing.

3. **Identify the KPIs and metrics.** Brainstorm the KPIs and metrics against which the different stakeholders will measure the effectiveness of the targeted initiative or decision. These KPIs and metrics should include financial, operational, stakeholder, partner, employee, environmental, and societal measures. It's important to note that these KPIs and metrics will play a critical role when you define your AI utility function.

4. **Instrument a decision-making process.** Ensure that the decision-making process is enabled with tags and sensors to monitor and identify performance anomalies, trends, and patterns, and make the necessary adjustments as quickly as possible.

5. **Create supporting aides and guides.** Leverage worksheets, checklists, and design templates to guide the brainstorming, monitoring, and measuring of potential unintended consequences process.

6. **Establish a formal review process.** Operationalize the decision-making process with formal and regular checkpoints that capture decision-making lessons and best practices, and analyze outcomes' effectiveness to avoid future unintended consequences.

The challenge in codifying ethics into laws and regulations is the lag effect that can occur due to rapid technological and cultural advancements, which can quickly render the laws ineffective. Consequently, the design and implementation of laws and regulations must be continuously monitored, measured, and adjusted based on what we learn from the effectiveness of those laws and regulations to drive the right behaviors and outcomes (interesting, because that's exactly how AI works).

Summary

This chapter brought together all the different concepts that we have discussed intending to define, design, develop, and implement AI models that deliver meaningful, relevant, responsible, and ethical outcomes. In this chapter, we provided a foundational definition of ethics upon which to base the ethical AI conversation and highlighted the powerful, if not unusual, relationship between economics and ethics. We then explored the potentially dire impact of the unintended consequences of AI implementations and, finally, introduced the Ethical AI Pyramid to guide the implementation of AI that aligns with and reinforces our societal laws and norms.

All this discussion about how we can build AI models that deliver meaningful, relevant, responsible, and ethical outcomes has got me thinking about the bigger societal ramifications. What would be the ramifications to society if we paid our leaders based on the metrics that mattered most? How would that change the laws and regulations that were written, the actions that leadership took, and the decisions that government and social agencies made?

Here's an interesting point to contemplate: while we can go through this detailed process to create AI models that act ethically, what are we doing to solve the bigger problem of creating incentive systems to get humans to act ethically?

That one is on all of us to become better humans...

In the next chapter, we are going to talk about the importance of individual and cultural empowerment. Yes, we are going to dedicate an entire chapter to helping people and organizations unleash their natural greatness through empowerment, fueling those natural human strengths to ensure that AI models deliver meaningful, relevant, responsible, and ethical outcomes. A perfect capstone to one's AI and data literacy journey!

References

1. Project Bread. *School Meals for All Saves $152 Annually, According to New Tufts Research*: https://projectbread.org/blog/school-meals-for-all-saves-152-annually-according-to-new-tufts-research

2. *High Return on Investment (ROI)*: https://www.impact.upenn.edu/early-childhood-toolkit/why-invest/what-is-the-return-on-investment/

3. Bernie Madoff: https://www.investopedia.com/terms/b/bernard-madoff.asp

4. Elizabeth Holmes and Theranos: https://www.bbc.com/news/business-58336998

5. Purdue Pharma and oxycontin: `https://www.ncbi.nlm.nih.gov/pmc/articles/PMC9339402/`

6. FTX crypto facade: `https://www.nationalreview.com/the-morning-jolt/what-you-need-to-know-about-the-colossal-mess-of-ftx/`

7. Des Moines Register. Mick Barry, *Bottle Bill is good for our state's environment and economy*: `https://www.desmoinesregister.com/story/opinion/columnists/iowa-view/2018/03/20/bottle-bill-good-our-states-environment-and-economy/441535002/`

8. Vukani Mngxati, *Responsible AI: A Framework for Building Trust*: `https://www.linkedin.com/pulse/responsible-ai-framework-building-trust-vukani-mngxati/`

9. Scott M. Lundberg and Sun-In Lee, *A Unified Approach to Interpreting Model Predictions*: `https://papers.nips.cc/paper/2017/file/8a20a8621978632d76c43dfd28b67767-Paper.pdf`

Join our book's Discord space

Join our Discord community to meet like-minded people and learn alongside more than 4000 people at:

`https://packt.link/data`

9

Cultural Empowerment

In this chapter, we want to focus on the secret to successful AI and data literacy – empowering yourself and your people. This may well be the most challenging chapter in the book because it forces Citizens of Data Science to embrace a very uncomfortable and even troubling concept – ambiguity.

Ambiguity – the quality of being open to more than one interpretation – is the key to human, society, and organizational evolution. If everyone has the same perspectives and same opinions, if our thinking is just a clone of everyone else's thinking, then human evolution and growth are over, and AI will win.

To quote popular American self-help author Peter McWilliams:

> *"Be willing to be uncomfortable. Be comfortable being uncomfortable. It may get tough, but it's a small price to pay for living a dream."*

This chapter may be uncomfortable for some readers as it delves into the innate human tendency to gravitate toward individuals who share similar traits and perspectives. It is undeniably more convenient and comforting to work alongside like-minded individuals. However, such a homogeneous environment can inadvertently breed stagnation and, even more alarmingly, foster groupthink – a psychological phenomenon wherein the pursuit of harmony and conformity within a group undermines rational decision-making and yields unfavorable results.

This chapter builds on the ideas and concepts first presented in my previous book, *The Economics of Data, Analytics, and Digital Transformation*. Nothing we have discussed in this book makes a difference if people are not empowered; people following their natural curiosity fuels creativity and drives organizational and societal innovation. Yes, this is the book's most important chapter because nothing else matters without it.

This chapter provides a critical exploration of cultivating a culture that not only values but also actively nurtures the diversity of perspectives. This chapter focuses on empowering individuals and teams to embrace and leverage a wide range of viewpoints, propelling them toward the innovation necessary to successfully complete their AI and data literacy journey. By fostering an environment that celebrates and harnesses diverse perspectives, we can unlock the potential to drive profound change and embrace the opportunities presented by AI and data. Without empowerment, your AI and data literacy efforts will be for naught.

In a nutshell, the following topics will be covered in this chapter:

- A history lesson on team empowerment
- 6 tips for cultivating a culture of empowerment
- Driving AI and data literacy via cultural empowerment
- Reassessing your AI and data literacy

A history lesson on team empowerment

In the Battle of Trafalgar in 1805, Admiral Lord Nelson found himself confronted by the formidable combined naval armada of France and Spain. This unified force aimed to pave the way for Napoleon's invasion of England, with Lord Nelson being the sole obstacle in their path. Despite facing overwhelming numerical and firepower disadvantages, Lord Nelson recognized the need to redefine his battle strategy in order to overcome these significant hurdles.

During that era, the prevailing method of naval warfare involved ships forming parallel lines, maximizing the firing capabilities of their cannons. Naval battles were often reduced to a mathematical equation, where the side able to unleash a greater number of cannonballs in the shortest time held the advantage, and subsequently, victory. However, Lord Nelson realized that a different approach was necessary to secure success in this dire situation.

Given his position as the underdog, Lord Nelson decided on a different naval engagement strategy. Instead of the traditional parallel arrangement, he arranged his ships perpendicularly and drove them directly into the French and Spanish Armada's line. This approach, captured in *Figure 9.1*, minimized the enemy's firepower advantage (a less exposed surface area for Lord Nelson's fleet to endure more cannon damage).

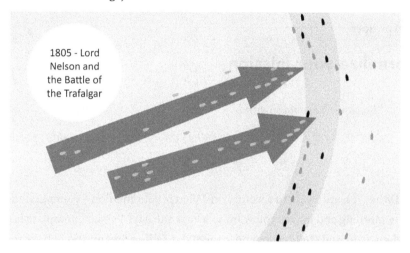

Figure 9.1: Lord Nelson and the Battle of the Trafalgar

A lot of credit for Lord Nelson's overwhelming success in the naval battle was given to his innovative battle strategy, but more important to his success was how he empowered each ship captain to operate independently during the heat of battle, effectively turning each ship captain into an *entrepreneur of battle.*

On the opposite side, the French and Spanish Armada was commanded by Vice Admiral Pierre-Charles de Villeneuve and Admiral Don Federico Gravina. They used the traditional, centralized command-and-control structure to send battle instructions (using flags) to the Armada ship captains with instructions on how to proceed during the battle.

Lord Nelson exploited his decentralized, empowered team approach to defeat the centralized command-and-control structure of the French and Spanish Armada. In fact, Lord Nelson's captains successfully won the battle even though Lord Nelson was killed during the battle.

So, what can we learn from Lord Nelson and the Battle of the Trafalgar? That data and AI literacy start with empowerment. But how can we master empowerment?

Tips for cultivating a culture of empowerment

Let's provide some tips on how management at any level can create an empowered organization. These tips can not only help your organization survive but can prepare your organization to thrive in today's time of constant change and transformation. With an empowered organization, Citizens of Data Science are now prepared to transform problems and challenges into opportunities to grow and prosper.

#1: Internalize your mission

"Begin with an end in mind."

— Stephen Covey, 7 Habits of Highly Effective People

Understand what you are trying to accomplish. What is your mission – your passion? What fires you up in the morning and makes you want to attack the day? Then contemplate how it creates value for others (e.g., stakeholders or constituents). Leading organizations have mission statements – brief statements or phrases that clearly articulate why the organization exists.

Here are some of my favorite mission statements:

- TED: Spread ideas.
- JetBlue: To inspire humanity in the air and on the ground.
- American Heart Association: To be a relentless force for a world of longer, healthier lives.
- Patagonia: Build the best product, cause no unnecessary harm, and use business to inspire and implement solutions to the environmental crisis.
- Nordstrom: To give customers the most compelling shopping experience possible.
- LinkedIn: Create economic opportunity for every member of the global workforce.
- Starbucks: To inspire and nurture the human spirit—one person, one cup, and one neighborhood at a time.

Empowerment starts by understanding and articulating your personal mission statement. I suspect Lord Nelson's mission statement was probably very simple: "Don't let the French break through our line; otherwise, we're going to be eating baguettes instead of fish and chips." A bit lengthy, but I bet it was something like that.

What is my mission statement? "Give back, mentor others, and share what I have learned."

I have been blessed with many mentors throughout my life and have been fortunate to have many Forrest Gump moments of being at the right place at the right time… not because I'm tall, good-looking, and from Iowa, but sometimes we just get lucky. So, I earnestly believe it's important for me to give back considering everything that has been given to me.

#2: Walk in the shoes of your stakeholders

Focus on serving your stakeholders and constituents. We will leverage a concept called design thinking to better understand our stakeholders and constituents (their intentions, objectives, desired outcomes, and key decisions) so that we can serve them better.

Design thinking is a stakeholder-centric approach that requires an open and collaborative mindset to discover and validate stakeholder needs and desired outcomes. Design thinking is a highly iterative process that starts with empathizing with the stakeholder's objectives, determining the stakeholder's intentions and desired outcomes (in other words, empathizing with them), ideating potential solutions (where all ideas are worthy of consideration), prototyping different solution options (to validate and learn from our stakeholders), and testing, learning, and refining until you find a solution that's viable and compelling for your stakeholders.

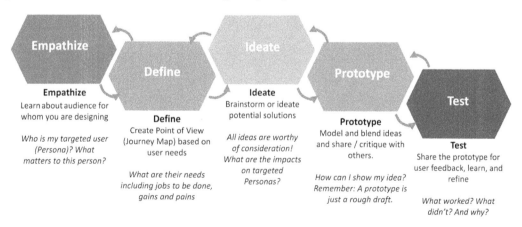

Figure 9.2: Design thinking – speaking the language of your customers

Design thinking uses a variety of design tools to intimate and understand your customers and stakeholders, including:

- **Persona profiles** to personalize or humanize our customers and stakeholders, including their intentions, goals, objectives, and desired outcomes

- **Journey maps** to understand the customer or stakeholder's journey toward those desired outcomes, key decisions, and the KPIs and metrics against which they will measure the outcomes and the decisions' effectiveness (the journey map also includes the associated benefits and impediments in completing the journey)

- **Stakeholder maps** that articulate each stakeholder's *win conditions*, needs, gains, and pain points

With those stakeholder insights in hand, we are ready to support our customers' journeys.

#3: Nurture organizational improvisation

Organizational improvisation yields flexible and malleable teams that can morph or transform in response to the changing needs of the situation. Like a great soccer team or jazz quartet, successful teams embrace organizational improvisation to get the most out of their people and unleash their natural greatness.

Teams are the driving force behind transformative change. While individuals can inspire and promote a compelling vision, it is ultimately empowered teams that emerge victorious. Thus, to foster such teams, it becomes crucial to master organizational improvisation.

How can we nurture empowered teams capable of adapting amid challenging situations, while simultaneously spearheading digital transformation in an ever-evolving landscape? One surprising source of inspiration can be found in playing video games!

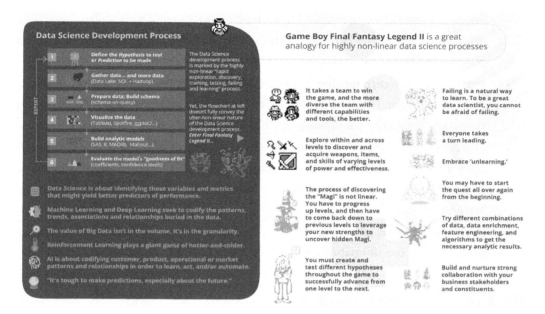

Figure 9.3: Cultural Transformation lessons courtesy of my Game Boy©

The Game Boy© Final Fantasy Legend II™ game is a surprising management tool that yields several valuable lessons in creating empowered teams, including:

- **It takes a team to win.** Winning requires a cohesive team with diverse perspectives and capabilities. When building your team, prioritize potential capabilities over current ones, investing in the team's future growth and potential.

- **Discovery is highly non-linear.** The journey of discovery isn't a straight line; it often necessitates revisiting and gathering insights that were initially overlooked or that you just weren't prepared to understand. Embrace the flexibility to double back as the journey dictates.

- **Continuously build and test hypotheses.** Continuously build and test hypotheses, exploring a multitude of possibilities to identify the winning ones. Success is achieved by defining, testing, proving, and advancing hypotheses one by one, with each success informing the development of the next hypothesis.

- **Failing is a natural way to learn.** Embrace failure as a natural part of the learning process. Every interaction provides a learning opportunity, and failures offer valuable insights into personal and team deficiencies. Embrace failure as a catalyst for growth and learning.

- **Everyone takes a turn leading.** Prepare every team member to lead. Ensure everyone receives training and feels empowered to lead, fostering a culture where everyone is ready to step up when their turn comes.

- **Embrace unlearning.** Skills and capabilities that served you in the past may prove inadequate in new situations. Be open to letting go of or unlearning outdated approaches and embracing new ones as you encounter different obstacles and challenges along your journey.

- **Be prepared to start all over.** Sometimes, your current strategy reaches its limits, necessitating a team transformation with different perspectives, capabilities, and experiences. Nurturing organizational improvisation becomes crucial to successfully navigating such transitions.

- **Embrace diversity of perspectives.** Blend, bend, and break apart different perspectives to overcome challenges. Surprisingly valuable and actionable insights often emerge from unexpected combinations.

- **Nurture strong collaboration across your ecosystem.** Finally, nurture strong collaboration between stakeholders and constituents who may play crucial roles at critical points in your journey. Building and maintaining robust relationships across your ecosystem strengthens your team and significantly improves your chances of success.

So, dust off that old Game Boy and learn how to master empowerment!

#4: Embrace an "AND" mentality

Without friction, there is no traction or progress.

One of the most important organizational conditions in enabling cultural empowerment is around the transition from an "OR" mentality to an "AND" mentality.

The "OR" mentality involves making choices and trade-offs between mutually exclusive options, prioritizing one while sacrificing others. It operates under the assumption of limited scope and zero-sum thinking, focusing on selecting the best single option while disregarding alternatives.

On the other hand, the "AND" mentality seeks to integrate multiple options, ideas, or conditions simultaneously, aiming for comprehensive and inclusive solutions. It explores synergies, embraces diverse perspectives, encourages collaboration, and fosters creative problem-solving. The "AND" mentality expands possibilities and goes beyond binary choices, while the "OR" mentality emphasizes exclusivity and prioritization.

Another history lesson. If you had challenged car manufacturers in 1979 to increase horsepower while improving mileage per car, the automobile executives would have looked at you like you had lobsters crawling out of your ears. However, that is precisely what happened.

In 1975, the US federal government mandated the **Corporate Average Fuel Economy (CAFE)** standards for automakers to make engines more efficient. Traditionally, car manufacturers provided an *OR* option – customers could have cars with good fuel mileage *or* horsepower but not both. So, to meet CAFE standards, car manufacturers in **Phase 1** of *Figure 9.4* started to cut horsepower to reach mileage goals. Then, around 1985, there was an industrial transformation (**Phase 2** of *Figure 9.4*) in which car manufacturers embraced the conflict between mileage and horsepower. They explored many different ideas, not all of which succeeded (see the note on the Wankel engine) in an attempt to improve mileage *and* horsepower. This was an era of great product design, development, and manufacturing creativity and innovation. Then, around 2008 (around the time of Tesla's first electric vehicle), the industry fully embraced the concept of horsepower *and* mileage. The result: cars with very high horsepower and infinite mileage (the 1020-hp Tesla tri-motor Plaid performance model gets to 60 mph in just 2.1 seconds, running only on batteries).

 The Wankel engine is an internal combustion engine that uses an eccentric rotary design to convert pressure into rotating motion. However, it had a lower thermal efficiency and poorer exhaust gas behavior compared to traditional engines, which led to its failure.

Instead of going out of business, car manufacturers embraced an "AND" mentality and ended up both improving fuel mileage *and* increasing horsepower through several product design, development, and manufacturing innovations (see *Figure 9.4*).

Embrace Diversity and Conflict to Fuel Innovation

Leading organizations' fuel innovation by seeking to optimize operational performance across conflicting conditions

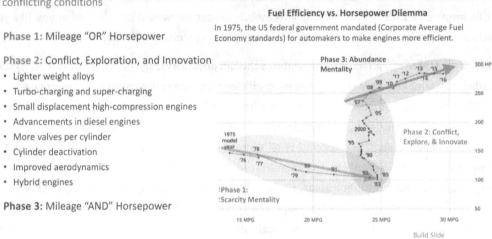

Phase 1: Mileage "OR" Horsepower

Phase 2: Conflict, Exploration, and Innovation

- Lighter weight alloys
- Turbo-charging and super-charging
- Small displacement high-compression engines
- Advancements in diesel engines
- More valves per cylinder
- Cylinder deactivation
- Improved aerodynamics
- Hybrid engines

Phase 3: Mileage "AND" Horsepower

Fuel Efficiency vs. Horsepower Dilemma

In 1975, the US federal government mandated (Corporate Average Fuel Economy standards) for automakers to make engines more efficient.

Figure 9.4: Economic Transformation of the Automobile Industry

Citizens of Data Science must replace their "OR" mentality with an "AND" mentality. This "AND" mentality exploits the different perspectives of different stakeholders to synergize and create something better than the original.

When diverse stakeholders are empowered to identify, share, and integrate their varied perspectives, organizations can transform their operational decision-making from the least *worst option* into the best *best option*.

Citizens of Data Science can transition from the least *worst options* to the best *best options* by understanding everyone's perspectives and rationale. These perspectives and rationale can be blended, integrated, and synergized to create the best *best option*.

You'll be surprised how enlightening and fun it can be when you seek to transform everyone's different perspectives and rationale into new, more innovative solutions.

#5: Ensure everyone has a voice

All ideas are worthy of consideration.

There may not be a more powerful and more straightforward ideation concept than *"all ideas are worthy of consideration."* Now, let's be clear. Not all ideas are good or worthy of action. But if you start filtering ideas during the ideation and empowerment process, you might never get the best ideas on the table.

If people feel that their ideas are welcome, you'll have a flood of new ideas. And open and free-form ideation builds upon itself, leading to permutations and synergies of existing ideas and new ideas. Yes, ideation is contagious when everyone feels free to voice their ideas and thoughts without judgment.

To reiterate what we established in *Chapter 3*, if you don't have enough *might* moments, you'll never have any breakthrough ideas.

Breakthrough ideas thrive on *might* moments. These moments of uncertainty and exploration are crucial for generating innovative or breakthrough solutions. By embracing ideas that might be useful, even without certainty, you open the door to creative possibilities and breakthrough thinking.

Might is a powerful enabler. It represents ideas with potential value, despite uncertain outcomes. Embracing the concept of *might* allows you to step beyond known solutions and explore uncharted territories, fostering an environment for innovative thinking and breakthrough ideas.

Ideation's power lies in a bounty of potential ideas that *might* yield new solutions. The process of generating ideas becomes more effective when there is a diverse range of possibilities to explore. Each *might* moment represents an opportunity for exploration and experimentation, increasing the chances of discovering transformative ideas.

These beliefs are the foundation for the growth mindset that every leader must embrace if they genuinely seek to unleash their employees' greatness.

And that's the real power of a culture of empowerment and ideation; your best ideas will likely come from the folks at the front lines of the organization – those employees engaging daily with your customers and the operations of the business.

#6: Unleash the curiosity-creativity-innovation pyramid

As we discussed earlier, AI is a learning technology capable of optimizing decisions and actions within a real-world environment. However, to reach the pinnacle of empowerment, we must move beyond optimization to reinvention and innovation. It's not sufficient to "optimize the cowpath" (that's the good old Iowa boy in me coming out). Instead, we must seek to "reinvent the cowpath."

To reinvent and innovate, we must embrace the most basic human trait – curiosity – the one trait that differentiates humans from machines. Curiosity is the foundation that powers the curiosity-creativity-innovation pyramid. Here's an illustration:

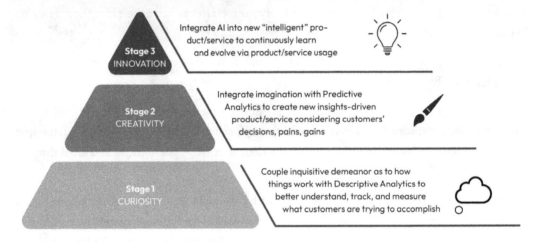

Figure 9.5: Organizational empowerment – creating a path from optimization to innovation

The path to reinvention and innovation starts by nurturing our natural curiosity; that natural tendency to explore, experiment, and try new things. Despite the fact that humans are born with natural curiosity and creativity, advantages not possessed by algorithms (such as the urge to disassemble and explore your dad's radio... a regrettable decision), a notable hurdle arises in the inclination of businesses and educational institutions to suppress curiosity. As a society, we seem to do everything in our power to erase that natural human curiosity – we have standardized classrooms, standardized curriculums, standardized tests, standardized job descriptions, standardized operating procedures, and standardized promotion schedules.

Standardization was necessary to solve many of society's fundamental problems. But the problem today is that AI will master optimization better than humans. In a world of AI-fueled products, humans must build a culture that nurtures curiosity and exploration to differentiate ourselves from our AI brethren.

Driving AI and data literacy via cultural empowerment

Cultural empowerment is the catalyst for mastering AI and data literacy. By embracing cultural empowerment, we cultivate a growth mindset that recognizes the significance of data and analytics as strategic assets capable of driving innovation, informed decision-making, and value creation. Moreover, the cultivation of AI and data literacy equips individuals with the knowledge to exploit AI and data within their specific areas of expertise and interest. This includes understanding how your personal data is collected, the analytic techniques used to uncover the behavioral patterns that shape your decisions and actions, and the capacity to utilize AI and data in a manner that produces meaningful, relevant, responsible, and ethically sound outcomes.

The relationship between cultural empowerment and AI and data literacy is symbiotic, with each reinforcing the other. An organization that fosters empowerment has profound effects on morale, collaboration, collective learning, confidence, and overall competitiveness. Simultaneously, employees equipped with AI and data literacy skills can actively contribute to the culture of data citizenship that drives innovation and facilitates responsible and ethical value creation.

Empowerment is the key, and to become a citizen of data science, it is your responsibility and obligation to be empowered...

- Empowered to have a voice
- Empowered to be treated as an equal, where all ideas are worthy of consideration
- Empowered to practice critical thinking, think for yourself, and challenge what others are telling you
- Empowered to be wrong, and to try, fail, learn, and try again
- Empowered to ask for the rationale and assumptions that power the decisions that impact you and others
- Empowered to ask more of your leaders and demand they take measures that benefit everyone, not just the measures that benefit them
- Empowered to ensure that everyone is being heard and has a seat at the table
- Empowered to demand ethical treatment and embrace the Golden Rule – to treat everyone as you would like to be treated – as fundamental to all interactions
- Empowered to raise your hand and say "I don't get it!"
- Empowered to confront and synergize, not to run away and sulk when you don't like what you hear

- Empowered to hold others accountable for their actions, but also empowered to hold yourself accountable for your actions
- Empowered to admit when you are wrong and make a mistake, and say that you are sorry
- Empowered to help others, to do good, and to share your good fortune
- Empowered to forgive others and then move on
- Empowered to think and act spiritually and ethically

Empowerment is proactive. It's not something that someone can just give you. To become an empowered citizen of life, you must courageously seize it for yourself. Pointing fingers and blaming others is futile and just surrenders your power, for the path to empowerment rests solely in your hands.

Now, the moment has arrived to consolidate and evaluate the valuable insights we have acquired throughout this book. We must combine our newfound knowledge to prepare ourselves for the pivotal responsibility we have in guaranteeing the ethical design, development, and management of AI.

Although I am not particularly fond of administering tests, there are certain occasions when tests become absolutely imperative in assessing our level of readiness. In this case, this particular assessment serves as a critical juncture, ensuring that we are adequately prepared to embrace our role as Citizens of Data Science.

Reassessing your AI and data literacy

Remember the AI and data literacy radar chart we introduced at the end of *Chapter 1*? We began our AI and data literacy journey by using that chart to assess how prepared we were to leverage AI and data literacy to become a Citizen of Data Science and to understand our role and the necessary capabilities to ensure the delivery of meaningful, relevant, responsible, and ethical AI outcomes.

Let's now take the opportunity to reassess our AI and data literacy scores as measured in the AI and data literacy radar chart, now that we have completed all the chapters in the book. Hopefully, your scores across all six dimensions will have improved. If not, then you might want to re-review specific chapters and take the assessment again. For ease of reference, we have included the AI and data literacy radar chart here:

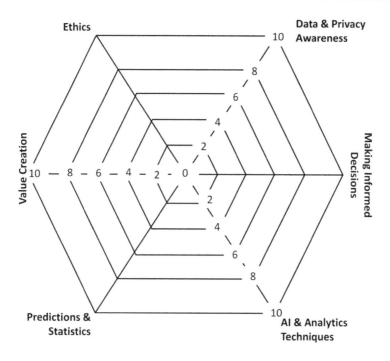

Figure 9.6: AI and data literacy radar chart

As a refresher, here are the key teachings from the book and their application to each of the key components of AI and data literacy as highlighted in the AI and data literacy radar chart:

- **Data and Privacy Awareness**: Understanding where and how your personal data is captured and used to influence how you think and act. In *Chapter 2*, we sought to answer the following questions: do you understand the ramifications of the transition from data to big data? Do you understand all the different situations and scenarios in which organizations are capturing your personal data? Do you understand how companies are mining your personal data to influence your actions, decisions, and beliefs? Do you understand the goals and limitations of data privacy laws and legislation?

- **AI and Analytic Techniques**: Understanding the wide range of advanced analytic algorithms (with a special focus on AI), and how to apply these algorithms to make more informed decisions. In *Chapters 3* and *4*, we sought to address the following questions: do you understand the capability differences between traditional business intelligence and data science? Do you understand the wide range of analytic algorithms, and how they are used to report, optimize, and learn? Do you understand how AI works and the critically important role of the AI utility function? Do you understand the role that you play in ensuring the development of a healthy and ethical AI utility function?

- **Making Informed Decisions:** Understanding how we can leverage data and analytics to make "models" to guide decision-making in order to make more informed decisions. In *Chapter 5*, we explored the following questions: do you know how to identify common decision-making traps, and what you can do to avoid those traps? Do you understand how to use a Decision Matrix to provide a framework for making more informed decisions? Could you teach someone the important points that comprise critical thinking?

- **Predictions and Statistics:** Understanding how to use basic statistical concepts to make predictions about what is likely to happen next, which enables informed decision-making. In *Chapter 6*, we sought to answer the following questions: do you understand how to apply some fundamental statistical concepts such as the mean, variance, confidence levels, and confusion matrix? Do you understand the fundamental differences between leading and lagging indicators and the associated risks of optimizing lagging indicators? Do you understand AI model false positives and false negatives, and the role they play in combatting AI model confirmation bias?

- **Value Creation:** Understanding how organizations leverage data and analytics to create "value." In *Chapter 7*, we sought to answer the following questions: do you understand the critical value creation differences between finance and economics? Do you understand how to use the Data and AI Analytics Business Model Maturity Index to measure how effective your organization is at leveraging data and analytics to power your business models? Do you understand how to identify your organization's value creation processes and the variables and metrics against which value creation effectiveness is measured? Do you understand the game-changing ramifications of the economies of learning?

- **AI Ethics:** Understanding the moral principles of right and wrong that govern a person's behavior or actions and their critical role in defining healthy, ethical AI utility functions. In *Chapter 8*, we sought to answer the following questions: do you understand what constitutes ethics? Do you understand the unusual but pivotal relationship between ethics and economics? Do you understand the dangers of unintended consequences and the assessment worksheet that can help organizations identify, monitor, and avoid these potentially dire unintended consequences? Do you understand how to leverage the AI Ethics Pyramid to guide the organization in the design, development, and implementation of responsible and ethical AI models?

I think we are now ready to retake the AI and Data Literacy assessment. I've included the guidelines in the following table to help you complete your AI and data literacy radar chart:

Category	Low	Medium	High
Data and privacy awareness	Just click and accept the website and mobile app's terms and conditions without reading	Attempt to determine the credibility of the site or app before accepting the terms and downloading	Read website and mobile app privacy terms and conditions and validate app and site credibility before engaging
Informed decision-making	Depend on their favorite TV channel, celebrities, or website to tell them what to think; prone to conspiracy theories	Research issues before making a decision, though still overweigh the opinions of people who "think like me"	Create a model that considers false positives and false negatives before making a decision; practice critical thinking
AI and analytic techniques	Believe that AI is something only applicable to large organizations and three-letter government agencies	Understand how AI is part of a spectrum of analytics, but not sure what each analytic technique can do	Understand how to collaborate to identify KPIs and metrics across a wide variety of value dimensions that comprise the AI utility function
Predictions and statistics	Don't seek to understand the probabilities of events happening; blind to unintended consequences of decisions	Do consider probabilities when making decisions but carry out a thorough assessment of the potential unintended consequences	Actively seek out information from credible sources to improve the odds of making an informed decision
Value engineering competency	Don't understand the dimensions of "value"	Understand the value dimensions but haven't identified the KPIs and metrics against which value creation effectiveness is measured	Understand the value dimensions and have identified the KPIs and metrics against which value creation effectiveness is measured
Ethics	Think ethics is something that only applies to "others"	Acknowledge the importance of ethics but are not sure how best to address it	Proactively contemplate different perspectives to ensure ethical decisions and actions

Table 9.1: AI and data literacy radar guidelines chart

Hopefully, you made progress in improving your AI and data literacy across the different categories of literacy. For those areas in which you didn't make the progress you would have liked to make, well, you might want to re-read and study the associated chapters.

Summary

As you have seen in this chapter, creating Citizens of Data Science requires empowering everyone in an organization and giving everyone a voice in where and how AI is designed and deployed to drive meaningful, relevant, responsible, and ethical outcomes.

That means we need to celebrate our personal mission and walk in the shoes of our stakeholders and constituents. We need to embrace an "AND" mentality and foster the organizational improvisation necessary to put people in the right places so they can be successful and grow. Ultimately, Citizens of Data Science must nurture their natural human traits of curiosity, creativity, and innovation to thrive in a world more and more dominated by AI and data. You have all the tools and skills necessary to succeed, but your success is ultimately on you. The minute you start to blame others for your problems, you abdicate control of your life. Own your mistakes, and you will own your future.

In the upcoming final chapter, we will put the AI and data literacy learnings to the test, evaluating their effectiveness against the most significant technological advancements of our time: ChatGPT, Bing, and Bard, powered by GenAI and LLMs.

These cutting-edge technologies have sparked both awe and apprehension regarding the vast potential of AI, fueling concerns about potential harm to humanity. Yes, these new technologies provide a marvelous opportunity to apply the knowledge we have gained throughout this book and assess its practicality.

Join our book's Discord space

Join our Discord community to meet like-minded people and learn alongside more than 4000 people at:

`https://packt.link/data`

10

ChatGPT Changes Everything

"The Horror. The Horror."

– Colonel Walter E. Kurtz (Marlon Brando), Apocalypse Now

During the writing of this book, a technological revolution exploded unto the scene with the advent of **Generative AI (GenAI)**, ChatGPT, and **Large Language Models (LLMs)**. These cutting-edge advancements brought to life the promises and fears surrounding AI, captivating the public's imagination. The astounding popularity and rapid adoption of OpenAI's ChatGPT were unimaginable. People marveled at its human-like ability to respond to a vast range of questions, unleashing their creativity as they sought ChatGPT's assistance in crafting poems, love letters in the style of Romeo, legal briefs, and even blog posts.

However, amid the excitement, there was an undercurrent of trepidation fueled by popular movies like *The Terminator*, *Eagle Eye*, *I, Robot*, and *The Matrix*, which predicted ominous AI consequences. This impending apprehension prompted leading AI advocates, corporate figures, and social leaders to urgently address the issue. Through open letters and media appearances, they urged political leaders to act and regulate the adoption of AI before it posed an irreversible threat to humanity. It was an epochal moment akin to the AI-driven equivalent of American physicist R. Robert Oppenheimer's pivotal role in nuclear history.

The sudden surge in public awareness regarding AI's immense power and inherent risks provided a unique opportunity to assess the relevance and applicability of the AI and data literacy concepts expounded in this book. Yes, ChatGPT changed everything by elevating the critical importance of AI and data Literacy to the forefront of global priorities overnight, demanding attention and understanding from all corners of society.

The GenAI that powers OpenAI's ChatGPT, Microsoft's Bing, and Google's Bard is changing users' expectations of how they can leverage and interact with AI and big data. Unlike previous AI usage scenarios that worked behind the scenes to optimize business and operational use cases such as GPS navigation, marketing campaigns, fraud detection, hiring, credit, and college applications, ChatGPT and its brethren – such as Microsoft Bing and Google Bard – are front and center, engaging in *intelligent* conversations with humans. And while these technologies may make mistakes today, we know that AI is a learning technology, and ChatGPT and other GenAI products will learn and grow exponentially.

These AI-powered intelligent chatbots have created a massive debate regarding what we should do to contain or control AI before it's too late. AI industry leaders such as Elon Musk, Steve Wozniak, and Andrew Yang have written letters to the AI communities and government leaders asking for a pause on large-scale AI experiments until more research has been done on the potential unintended consequences of broad-scale, untethered AI deployments[1].

In an article in the Wall Street Journal titled *ChatGPT Heralds an Intellectual Revolution*, Henry Kissinger, Eric Schmidt, and Daniel Huttenlocher get right to the point of the issue:

> *"Whereas the printing press caused a profusion of modern human thought, the new technology achieves its distillation and elaboration. In the process, **it creates a gap between human knowledge and human understanding.**"*

Why is this ChatGPT conversation so important? Because in the same way that the likes of Amazon, Netflix, Spotify, Google, Waze, and others changed users' expectations regarding how they wanted companies to provide meaningful and relevant product and service recommendations to them, ChatGPT will change how users research, explore, and consume knowledge that could have dramatic impacts on our personal and professional lives.

In this chapter, the term "ChatGPT" will be used generically to encompass OpenAI's ChatGPT, Microsoft's Bing, Google's Bard, and other AI-powered intelligent chatbots and agents. And while that may not be a fair reference given the amount of research and development being done by others, it was ChatGPT that stormed onto the scene, like Michael Myers in the movie *Halloween*, and changed everything.

At the end of this chapter, we will review how the AI and data literacy concepts covered throughout this book prepare us as Citizens of Data Science to participate in the responsible and ethical application of AI and GenAI. But before we can do that, we need a little primer on GenAI.

To sum up, this chapter will discuss the following crucial topics:

- What are ChatGPT and GenAI?
- How does ChatGPT work?
- Understanding critical ChatGPT-enabling technologies
- ChatGPT concerns and risks
- Thriving with GenAI
- AI, data literacy, and ChatGPT

What are ChatGPT and GenAI?

GenAI is an AI system that relies on unsupervised or semi-supervised learning algorithms to create new and original digital content (e.g., articles, program code, poetry, photographs, artwork, and music) by learning from existing data or content.

ChatGPT (GPT stands for Generative Pre-trained Transformer) is a GenAI chatbot launched by OpenAI in November 2022. It is built on OpenAI's GPT family of LLMs and fine-tuned with supervised and reinforcement learning techniques.

ChatGPT uses supervised learning to train its LLM. The supervised learning model uses the labeled data gleaned from websites and digital books to identify statistical language patterns buried in the massive data sets to train an LLM. The LLM then leverages these statistical language patterns and **Natural Language Processing (NLP)** to generate human-like responses.

ChatGPT also uses **Reinforcement Learning from Human Feedback (RLHF)** to continue to refine and enhance the relevance and accuracy of its language model based on human feedback. This enables ChatGPT to generate informative and engaging human-like responses.

As explained in *Chapter 4*, **Artificial General Intelligence (AGI)** refers to AI capable of understanding and learning any intellectual task a human being can do rather than being specialized to support a fixed set of operational use cases.

However, ChatGPT is not AGI, the holy grail of the AI community. And outside the world of science fiction, AGI does not exist... yet. But with enough collaboration, exploration, and learning, sometimes science *fiction* can become science *fact*.

How does ChatGPT work?

Prior to evaluating the practicality of the AI and data literacy insights provided in this book, it is essential to establish a clear understanding – at the time of writing this book – of how ChatGPT and other GenAI-powered chatbots function.

Given the potential complexity and rapid confusion that may arise, we will adopt a progressive approach to familiarize ourselves with ChatGPT's operations through the eyes of Beginner, Capable, and Proficient user profiles. Hopefully, this graduated exposure approach will facilitate comprehension without overwhelming the readers with technical details.

Beginner level 101

If I had to explain ChatGPT to a beginner – someone who has tried ChatGPT but does not have a technology background – I'd say that ChatGPT is a simple concept that does four things exceptionally well:

1. Analyzes specific sites on the public internet and creates a contextual knowledge base.

    For example, ChatGPT is trained on all recipes, ingredients, instructions, and expected outcomes on public cooking websites.

2. Determines relevant language usage patterns and relationships.

    In our cooking example, ChatGPT uses its AI brain to analyze all the cooking websites to identify relevant patterns and relationships concerning recipes, ingredients, cooking instructions, and expected outcomes.

3. Parses user requests to determine user intent (better than most humans).

    In our cooking example, say my mother-in-law types in a request for a recipe. ChatGPT reads the request and uses its AI brain to determine my mother-in-law's intent and what she is asking.

4. Predicts what content is most relevant based on the user's intent.

    In our cooking example, based on the information and patterns that ChatGPT found on the cooking websites, ChatGPT recommends a recipe that it thinks my mother-in-law will like. This is like how auto-complete works in a search box or when writing a document, except ChatGPT is not auto-completing words; it is auto-completing sentences and paragraphs.

5. Formats a human-like response in presenting the content.

    In our cooking example, ChatGPT then writes a message in human-like language explaining the recipe and how to make it.

Now, if a more experienced person who had been doing some research on ChatGPT were to wander into the room and wanted to understand how ChatGPT works, I'd expand on each of the four tasks mentioned above.

Capable level 201

Level 201 is for someone who has done some reading and research on GenAI and LLMs. They have a solid understanding of what these technologies can do, but do not understand the underlying technologies and analytic processes that enable the amazing human-like outputs from the products that use these technologies.

1. ChatGPT analyzes and catalogs public data using a **transformer neural network** and **self-attention** to understand the context of the data based on the patterns and relationships from the data upon which it was trained. The results are stored in an LLM – a *knowledge repository* containing information patterns gleaned from the contextual information upon which ChatGPT was trained.

2. During training, ChatGPT learns to understand the patterns and relationships between words, phrases, and sentences in natural language by analyzing the statistical properties of the text data. ChatGPT uses the knowledge it has gained through training to generate a response statistically likely to be coherent and relevant to the input it has received.

3. ChatGPT uses NLP techniques to parse and understand user requests. It then accesses its knowledge repository to retrieve relevant information and generate a new response based on its understanding of the user's intent.

4. Once ChatGPT has determined the user's intent, it can search its LLM to predict the content most relevant to the user's request. This involves weighing various factors, such as the user's query, their query's context, and the content's relevance and quality, to generate a contextually relevant and informative response.

5. ChatGPT then generates a natural language response to present the information to the user. This involves selecting the appropriate words and phrasing to convey the information clearly and concisely, similar to how a human might respond to the user's request. ChatGPT employs a range of language generation techniques, such as paraphrasing, summarizing, or synthesizing information to present its response in a more accessible way.

However, even the 201 explanations only start to scratch the technology's complexity and the underlying mechanisms that power ChatGPT. Let's look at the more detailed 301 description.

Proficient level 301

The 301 proficient level is for those with experience in designing, developing, and deploying analytic models. These folks are comfortable with tools like Python and deep learning libraries and frameworks such as TensorFlow and PyTorch.

1. ChatGPT is an LLM trained on a massive amount of text data from publicly available data on the internet. It uses a Transformer architecture with billions of parameters that enable it to generate human-like responses to various prompts. This allows ChatGPT to understand the structure and syntax of the language and generate coherent sentences.

2. The transformer architecture is a type of neural network architecture introduced in the paper *Attention Is All You Need* by Vaswani et al. (2017). It is designed to process data sequences, such as text, and it uses self-attention to capture the dependencies between different parts of the sequence.

3. When a user submits a request to ChatGPT, the system uses NLP to understand the user's intent and parse the request. This involves breaking down the text into its parts, identifying the keywords and phrases, and interpreting the overall meaning of the request.

4. Once the request has been parsed, ChatGPT searches its internal knowledge base, which contains a vast amount of text data from the internet, including websites, social media posts, news articles, and other sources. The system uses machine learning algorithms to match the user request to relevant content in its database.

5. ChatGPT generates a response formatted to sound like a human-written response based on the matched content. ChatGPT uses a combination of NLP techniques and machine learning algorithms to generate human-like responses. Here are some of the techniques that ChatGPT uses:

   - NLP algorithms generate responses to user queries. These algorithms can generate natural and human-like text by modeling human language patterns and styles.

   - Contextual understanding to better understand the meaning behind user queries, such as the user's previous queries or the topic they are asking about, to generate more relevant and accurate responses.

   - Sentiment analysis to analyze the tone and sentiment of the text to generate appropriate and sensitive responses to the user's emotional state.

   - Summarization techniques to extract critical information from the text and present it concisely and understandably to provide users with easy-to-read and comprehensible information.

It's worth noting that ChatGPT is constantly learning and improving as it processes more user requests and gains access to more data. As discussed in *Chapter 4*, properly constructed AI models become more valuable the more they are used.

Now that we have an understanding of how ChatGPT works, let's explore some critical and unique ChatGPT technologies. While I do not want to get too technical, these technologies are the secret sauce for getting GenAI products to produce relevant, human-like responses.

Critical ChatGPT-enabling technologies

ChatGPT and other GenAI-powered chatbots leverage some unique technologies that are critical in enabling these GenAI products to deliver meaningful, relevant, responsible, and ethical outcomes. Understanding the basics of these technologies will help you be more effective when interacting with GenAI-powered products.

LLM

An LLM is an AI algorithm that can learn language patterns and relationships between words and phrases in textual data. It uses those patterns and relationships to predict a given context's next word or phrase.

LLMs are the backbone of GenAI chatbots. Key aspects and concerns of an LLM include:

- **Training data**: LLMs are trained on vast amounts of text data, such as digital books, articles, and web pages. The LLM uses this data to learn patterns in language (words and positions of words in sentences, paragraphs, and articles) and develop the ability to understand and generate human-like text.
- **NLP**: These intelligent AI chatbots leverage an NLP system to understand and generate human-like language.
- **Applications**: LLMs have a wide range of applications, including language translation, content generation, text summarization, language generation, answering questions, and more.
- **Architecture**: LLMs use deep learning algorithms like neural networks to analyze and generate text. They are often designed to be highly scalable, with the ability to quickly process vast amounts of data.

The tight collaboration between NLP and the LLM is vital in enabling ChatGPT to deliver relevant human-like responses to users. ChatGPT uses NLP to process the user request to understand the intent, context, and sentiment. The NLP system then utilizes the LLM to generate a response passed to ChatGPT.

ChatGPT takes the response generated by the LLM and further refines the response using machine learning algorithms to provide a more personalized and contextually relevant response to the user. After ChatGPT generates the response, the feedback loop collects data on the user's response, including whether the response was helpful or not. This data is then used to update and improve the accuracy and relevance of the LLM.

This flow is visualized in the following figure:

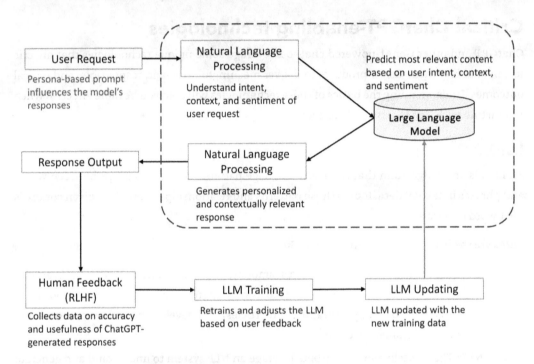

Figure 10.1: Role of LLMs in ChatGPT engagement

The LLM architecture typically includes these key components:

1. **Input encoding**: The input encoding component of an LLM is responsible for converting the raw input text into a numerical format that the model can process. This often involves techniques such as tokenization and embedding.

2. **Transformer layers**: Transformer layers are a crucial component of LLM architecture. They are designed to process the input text and generate context-aware representations of the text, which can be used for a wide range of NLP tasks.

3. **Attention mechanisms**: Attention mechanisms are used in LLMs to help the model focus on the most relevant parts of the input text. This is particularly important for long text sequences, where the model needs to selectively attend to the most important information.

4. **Decoding**: The decoding component of an LLM is responsible for generating output text based on the input and the internal representations developed by the model. This may involve techniques such as beam search or sampling.

5. **Fine-tuning**: Fine-tuning is essential to LLM architecture, particularly for transfer learning applications. It involves training the model on a specific task or domain, using a smaller amount of task-specific data, to optimize the model's performance for that particular task.

The following figure provides a high-level overview of these LLM components and the flow and interactions between these components to produce relevant responses to the user's request:

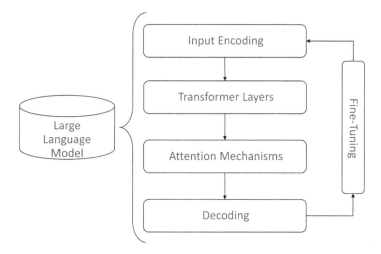

Figure 10.2: LLM key architecture components

LLMs have raised ethical concerns, particularly with bias and fairness issues. As AI becomes more advanced, it is essential to ensure that LLMs are designed and trained in a way that is ethical, transparent, and aligned with societal values.

Next, let's review one of the critical underlying technologies – deep learning transformers – and how they leverage self-attention to generate more relevant responses.

Transformers

A transformer is a type of deep learning model architecture that has revolutionized the field of NLP. It was introduced in the paper *Attention Is All You Need* by Vaswani et al. in 2017. You are probably already familiar with transformers since they enable the text and sentence auto-complete that we use in our web searches and many word processing applications.

Transformers excel at capturing long-range dependencies in sequences, which is crucial for understanding and generating coherent and contextually relevant responses. The key component of transformers is the attention mechanism, which allows the model to isolate and focus on different parts of the input sequence when generating the output.

Transformers enable the GenAI model to learn contextual representations of words and sentences, capturing both local and overall relationships within the input text. By isolating the relevant parts of the conversation history, transformers can generate responses that take into account the broader context and produce more coherent and contextually appropriate replies.

Additionally, transformers use a technique called self-attention, where each word pays attention to other words in the text, allowing the model to decide which words are more important given the context of the input request. This helps the model to understand how words depend on and relate to each other, which is vital for making meaningful replies.

Finally, let's talk about the importance of personas in crafting prompts that deliver responses that are more relevant to you.

Role-based personas

A **role-based persona** represents a specific job or role used to understand the needs and behaviors of individuals in that role for better decision-making and strategy development. Role-based personas are the secret sauce enabling ChatGPT to deliver highly relevant responses.

ChatGPT leverages several techniques to create role-based personas that yield more relevant responses and are the heart of ChatGPT's continuous learning capabilities. These role-based persona techniques are listed here:

- ChatGPT analyzes the input text and identifies the user's role (e.g., student, customer, patient, or software developer) and intent, which will guide the subsequent response and conversation. The user's role determines the persona that ChatGPT adopts for the system, as well as the tone, style, and level of formality of its responses. ChatGPT uses personas to remember the context and rules of the conversation to fine-tune its responses.

It also uses RLHF to improve the quality and accuracy of its responses. ChatGPT learns from the ratings and rankings of its responses from the users to generate responses more likely to be preferred by humans.

- ChatGPT uses NLP to extract entities and relations from the user's input text and constructs a content graph based on the input text and its knowledge base. This content graph is a representation of the entities and their relationships that are relevant to the conversation topic. For example, if the topic is about movies, the content graph could include actors, directors, genres, ratings, reviews, etc. The content graph helps ChatGPT generate responses that are informative, coherent, and consistent with the facts.

- ChatGPT uses the role-based persona and the content graph to generate a response appropriate for the user's query. For example, if the user asks for a movie recommendation, ChatGPT could use its persona as a movie expert to suggest a movie based on the user's preferences and the content graph. ChatGPT could also use its movie expert persona to express its opinions or emotions about the movie, making the response more engaging and human-like.

- ChatGPT uses RLHF to improve the quality and accuracy of its responses. ChatGPT learns from the user feedback and updates the content graph as the conversation progresses, adding new information or modifying existing information based on the user's input.

Let's dive into the critical role of RLHF next as it is the pivotal catalyst that enables GenAI models like ChatGPT to continuously learn and evolve in providing more relevant and accurate responses to its users' information requests.

Reinforcement Learning from Human Feedback

RLHF is a training technique used to improve GenAI models by incorporating feedback from human evaluators. The initial GenAI model is trained using supervised learning with human-generated examples and then fine-tuned using reinforcement learning with human feedback.

During the reinforcement learning process, human evaluators provide feedback on the accuracy of the model's responses. The evaluators can rate and rank different responses based on their quality, relevance, and other predefined criteria. This feedback helps the model to learn from its mistakes and improve its responses over time.

This feedback is then used to further train and improve the effectiveness and relevance of the model. The model adjusts its parameters to increase the likelihood of generating responses that align with the feedback received from human evaluators. This iterative process of training, feedback, and refinement helps improve the model's performance, making its outputs more relevant, meaningful, and aligned with human preferences.

RLHF is the *secret sauce* to enabling GenAI models to continuously refine their responses courtesy of the following capabilities:

- **Iterative improvement**: RLHF enables an iterative process of learning and refinement. Initially, GenAI models are trained using supervised learning, where human AI trainers provide conversations and model-generated responses. This data forms the basis for reinforcement learning, allowing the model to learn from human feedback and adapt over time.

- **Feedback loop**: With RLHF, the GenAI model receives feedback from human AI trainers or users, which helps it understand which responses are desirable or undesirable. By incorporating this feedback, the GenAI model can adjust its behavior and generate more appropriate and contextually relevant responses.

- **Addressing ethical concerns**: RLHF provides a means to address ethical concerns that may arise during training. By keeping human trainers in the loop, biases, misinformation, or inappropriate outputs can be identified and rectified, promoting responsible GenAI development and usage.

- **Navigating open-ended conversations**: Reinforcement learning allows the GenAI model to navigate open-ended conversations where there may not be a single correct answer. By learning from human feedback, the GenAI model can adapt and generate responses that align better with human expectations and preferences.

- **Balancing exploration and exploitation**: RLHF strikes a balance between exploration and exploitation. The model explores different response strategies, receives feedback, and adjusts its behavior accordingly. This process enables the GenAI model to explore new ways of responding while leveraging the knowledge gained from previous interactions.

Incorporating RLHF enables GenAI models to learn from human expertise and deliver more accurate and desirable outputs, enhancing the overall user experience.

Having gained a solid understanding of the workings of GenAI products, including their enabling technologies, let's delve into the significant concerns and risks associated with GenAI. This exploration aims to clarify and address the growing apprehension surrounding these GenAI technologies.

ChatGPT concerns and risks

"There are known knowns. These are things we know that we know. There are known unknowns. That is to say, there are things that we know we don't know. But there are also unknown unknowns. There are things we don't know we don't know."

– Donald Rumsfeld

One of the major concerns surrounding GenAI products revolves around the vast realm of unknown possibilities. We are continuously exploring and devising innovative applications for GenAI products, but these new applications of GenAI aren't carefully crafted in an easy-to-read user manual. Our journey involves a continuous process of experimentation and learning, as we strive to uncover the untapped potential of GenAI.

Consequently, since we don't know what we don't know, extraordinary rigor must be employed to identify the potential unintended consequences of using AI-powered products like ChatGPT. With that said, there are some risks and concerns associated with GenAI products that we do already know and can proactively work to address in the GenAI design, development, and deployment stages. These known risks and concerns include:

- **Confirmation bias:** We have already seen grave consequences from the confirmation bias exhibited by poorly constructed AI models. We are becoming increasingly aware of how AI model confirmation bias can have a negative impact on lending and finance, housing, employment, criminal justice, and healthcare.

- **Unintended consequences:** Unintended consequences are unforeseen results of an action or decision. One way to address this issue is through group exploration across a diverse set of stakeholders in ideating the potential negative and positive outcomes of AI deployments.

- **Mental atrophy:** Atrophy is the gradual decline in effectiveness due to underuse. We see this in our physical abilities as we get older, and yes, the same thing can happen to our brains. We must continue to challenge our conventional thinking to keep our mental capabilities sharp. For example, trying to recall the name of an actor in a movie is a good exercise for improving your cognitive function.

- **Hallucinations:** Hallucinations occur when the GenAI model generates responses or outputs that are nonsensical, misleading, or completely fabricated, leading to unreliable and potentially harmful information. These hallucinations can contribute to problems such as the spread of misinformation and falsehoods, erosion of trust in AI, ethical concerns, legal liabilities, and the potential for social manipulation.

- **Intellectual property (IP) protection:** The primary concerns regarding IP protection with GenAI models are the ownership and control of generated content, as well as the potential risks of data exposure and the inadvertent disclosure of sensitive information, including trade secrets. Content creators like authors and artists are concerned that they may lose control over their original works and will not be fairly compensated for the unauthorized use or infringement by the GenAI models.

Now that we have covered the key enabling GenAI technologies, let's shift focus to how we can best use GenAI products in our everyday lives.

Thriving with GenAI

GenAI models will reward individuals who can apply knowledge rather than those who can memorize and regurgitate knowledge.

The definition of success is changing. No longer will memorization and regurgitation of knowledge be sufficient. Instead, success will be defined by people who know how to apply knowledge to deliver meaningful, relevant, and ethical business, operational, and societal outcomes.

The roles that will prosper and excel in a world of AI are the roles that integrate and blend an understanding of data and analytics with their areas of expertise by:

- Identifying (envisioning) where and how AI can be applied to their professions to deliver more meaningful, relevant, and ethical business and operational outcomes.

- Driving cross-organizational alignment and consensus on the variables, metrics, and desired outcomes against which AI effectiveness will be measured.

- Defining a comprehensive, healthy AI utility function to avoid confirmation bias and unintended consequences.

- Implementing AI-based solutions in a manner that is easy for users to understand and use.

- Instrumenting, monitoring, and measuring the AI model outcomes' effectiveness (actual versus predicted results).

- Adapting business and operational processes to exploit AI's ability to continuously learn and adapt.

- Creating a culture of personal and team empowerment where all voices are heard and respected in designing AI models – and a comprehensive, healthy AI utility function – that delivers relevant, meaningful, and ethical outcomes.

One example of the successful application of GenAI is the creation of personal GenAI assistants, or **Your Own Digital Assistant (YODA)**, to help guide your personal and operational analysis in making more informed decisions. YODA would act as your personal agent in assessing your current situation, analyzing your history of engagements and interactions, leveraging a worldwide knowledge repository of similar experiences and expertise, and recommending actions to make more informed, more relevant, and safer decisions.

For example, let's say that you are a technician for a manufacturing facility and you notice a problem with one of the plant's electric motors. You could engage YODA to help you identify, explore, and assess the potential sources for the problem, such as:

- A mechanical issue with the motor or its components, such as bearing failure or misalignment, can cause increased friction and vibration.

- A problem with the motor's load, such as an overload or an unbalanced load, can cause increased current and vibration but not affect the voltage.

- A problem with the motor's drive system, such as a malfunctioning **variable frequency drive (VFD)** or a problem with the power supply, can cause increased current but won't affect the voltage.

- A problem with the motor's control system, such as a malfunctioning control circuit or a problem with the motor's control settings, can cause increased current but won't affect the voltage.

With that, I hope you can envision where this might lead in helping people and organizations make more informed, more relevant, and safer decisions.

Finally, it's time to synthesize our knowledge of GenAI and apply the AI and data literacy concepts that we've learned throughout this book, empowering us to assess our readiness in effectively utilizing GenAI and becoming active Citizens of Data Science. By combining our understanding of GenAI's capabilities with the foundational skills we've developed in AI and data literacy, we can embark on a journey toward leveraging GenAI and AI's potential to uncover valuable insights and make informed decisions in an increasingly data-driven world.

AI, data literacy, and GenAI

Let's apply the AI and Data Literacy Framework introduced in *Chapter 1* to assess how our AI and data literacy education helps prepare us for a world where GenAI-powered chatbots like OpenAI's ChatGPT, Microsoft's Bing, and Google's Bard play a more significant role in our personal and professional lives.

As was explained in *Chapter 1*, the following table serves as a guide in evaluating the actions and attributes that exemplify a proficient Citizen of Data Science who has learned to master the transformative power of GenAI and general AI. The table captures the essence of the key AI and data literacy dimensions discussed throughout this book, shedding light on the diverse skill set and mindset required to navigate the ever-evolving landscape of GenAI and AI to support informed decision-making.

Hopefully, readers can gain a deeper understanding of the multifaceted responsibilities and competencies involved in harnessing GenAI and AI's potential, ultimately enabling them to become contributing Citizens of Data Science.

Category	Lowest Level of Proficiency	Average Level of Proficiency	Highest Level of Proficiency
Data and privacy awareness	Accepts whatever GenAI produces as fact without validation	Attempts to ascertain the reasonableness of what GenAI produces before acting	Practices critical thinking by asking GenAI for sources of the information aggregated by GenAI, then reads the website app privacy terms, and validates site credibility before engaging
Informed decision-making	Forms opinions and makes decisions based on whatever GenAI says without consideration of potential biases or unintended consequences	Researches GenAI's response before forming an opinion or making a decision, though does not always double-check or validate what GenAI says	Integrates GenAI-validated information into their decision-making models and considers false positives and false negatives before making a decision
AI and analytic techniques	Believes that GenAI is something only applicable to large organizations and 3-letter government agencies	Knows that GenAI is driven by AI, but has invested the time to understand how one can make GenAI work for them	Understands how GenAI works, the underlying technologies, and the associated confirmation bias and unintended consequence risks
Predictions and statistics	Doesn't seek to understand the probabilities of events happening; blind to the potential unintended consequences of what GenAI states	Does consider probabilities when making decisions using GenAI, but doesn't seek additional information to complement and validate what GenAI shared	Actively seeks out information from credible sources to complement GenAI-provided information to improve the odds of making an informed decision

Value cre-ation	Doesn't understand the dimensions of "value" with respect to interacting with GenAI, which could lead to confirmation bias and unintended consequences	Understands the value dimensions but hasn't fully fleshed out the KPIs and metrics against which GenAI model effectiveness, relevance, and accuracy should be measured	Understands the value dimensions and the KPIs and metrics against which GenAI value creation effectiveness should be measured considering the costs associated with AI model false positives and false negatives
Ethics	Thinks GenAI is self-monitoring its answers with respect to ethical responses	Acknowledges the importance of ethics but is not sure how to integrate ethical measures when interacting with GenAI	Masters prompt engineering to ensure GenAI integrates different perspectives and is addressing confirmation bias when using GenAI to help make more informed decisions

Table 10.1: Applying AI and data literacy benchmarks to ChatGPT

In summary, the proficient Citizen of Data Science, with respect to GenAI usage, does the following:

- From a data and privacy standpoint, the proficient data scientist exercises critical thinking by posing validation queries to GenAI regarding the sources of information utilized to substantiate its responses. They also review the privacy terms of website applications and verify the credibility of the sites before accepting GenAI's answer. Moreover, the proficient data scientist seeks alternative perspectives by cross-referencing the results with other GenAI products like OpenAI's ChatGPT, Microsoft's Bing, and Google's Bard, blending the different responses and ascertaining the reasonableness of the different responses.

- From a perspective of making well-informed decisions, the proficient data scientist constructs decision models that reflect a thorough assessment, taking into consideration the associated costs and risks of the potential actions, and incorporates the GenAI responses into the framework of that decision model. Furthermore, they meticulously examine the list of decision traps to ensure that the GenAI responses have circumvented those traps.

- From the standpoint of AI and analytics, the proficient data scientist ensures that the viewpoints of diverse stakeholders are incorporated into the design, development, and ongoing prompt engineering process when engaging with the GenAI model. The proficient data scientist also ensures that the GenAI responses are relevant, meaningful, easily comprehensible, and actionable.

- From the perspective of predictions and statistics, the proficient data scientist poses inquiries regarding the underlying statistical confidence of the GenAI responses. They persist in interacting with the GenAI tool, investigating the model's false positive and false negative rates, until they attain a satisfactory level of statistical confidence in the GenAI model's responses.

- From a value engineering standpoint, the proficient data scientist initiates the GenAI interaction by comprehending the objectives of the questions, the intended outcomes, and the KPIs and metrics that will gauge the effectiveness of the outcomes. Subsequently, they employ the outcomes of the GenAI conversation to identify potential operational use cases and determine the specific KPIs and measures against which to measure progress and success within those use cases.

- Finally, from an ethics perspective, the proficient data scientist explores a wide range of stakeholder personas through the GenAI persona role capabilities to identify the short-term and long-term variables and metrics against which these stakeholders should seek to measure the relevance, responsible, and ethical AI model outcomes.

Embracing these 6 dimensions of AI and data literacy can help ensure that you are using GenAI to your benefit and to guide your personal and professional development.

Summary

The bottom line is to treat GenAI-enabled products as hard-working but flawed research assistants. That means double-checking their work, questioning sources, asking second - and third - order exploratory questions via prompt engineering, dictating the metrics against which the outcome's effectiveness and accuracy will be measured, assessing the GenAI responses for confirmation bias and unintended consequence, and practicing critical thinking before finally integrating the validated results from your GenAI partner to help you build more comprehensive decision models that power more informed decisions.

Much good can be realized from the potential of GenAI-powered chatbots to jump-start our thinking and challenge our assumptions. GenAI has already become a foundational piece in helping humans make informed decisions by forcing us to contemplate a more holistic range of factors and variables, challenge our long-held assumptions and biases, and move us to think versus respond.

But be aware. Becoming a Citizen of Data Science doesn't mean that your journey is now done or certification is now complete. As technologies evolve, so must the role of humans to leverage those technologies to create value. GenAI and future AI and data developments are only tools – but incredibly valuable tools that we must learn how to use to be more productive and effective.

Your journey to become a Citizen of Data Science isn't over; it's just starting. And it's on you to continue to use the AI and Data Literacy Framework outlined throughout this book to prepare yourself for a lifetime of exploring, learning, unlearning, and learning anew. With AI as your partner (and not your overlord), there is nothing you can't accomplish.

Best of luck!

References

1. *Pause Giant AI Experiments: An Open Letter*: `https://futureoflife.org/open-letter/pause-giant-ai-experiments/`

Join our book's Discord space

Join our Discord community to meet like-minded people and learn alongside more than 4000 people at:

`https://packt.link/data`

Glossary

Here are some terms that were used throughout the book.

Data economics

A **Data Economic Multiplier** is the accumulated attributable and quantifiable "value" from using a data set against multiple business or operational use cases.

The Economics is the branch of knowledge concerned with the production, consumption, and transfer of wealth or value.

Economic Multiplier Effect states that an injection of new spending (exports, government spending, or investment) can lead to an outsized increase in final national income (Gross Domestic Product).

Economies of Learning measure an organization's value creation effectiveness from continuously learning and adapting the organization's data and analytic assets based on business and operational interactions.

Economies of Scale are the cost advantages that enterprises obtain due to their scale of operation and are typically measured by the amount of output produced per unit of time.

An **Economic Value Curve** measures the relationship between dependent and independent variables to achieve a particular outcome.

A **Hypothesis Development Canvas** captures data science requirements, including business objectives and the KPIs and metrics against which to measure success, critical decisions by key stakeholders, potential ML features, and the costs of false positives and false negatives.

The Law of Accelerating Returns states that the human and cultural learnings from technology advancements feed on themselves, thereby accelerating the rate of advancement and pushing the overall technology advancements well past the linear extrapolation of current progress.

The Law of Diminishing Returns states that profits or benefits from something will represent a proportionally smaller gain as more money or energy is invested.

Marginal Cost is the cost added by producing one additional unit of a product or service.

Marginal Propensity to Consume (MPC) is the proportion of an increase in available funds spent on the consumption of goods and services instead of being saved.

Marginal Propensity to Reuse (MPR) states that an increase in the reuse of a data set across multiple use cases drives an increase in the attributable value of that data set at zero marginal cost.

Marginal Revenue is the revenue gained by producing one additional unit of a good or service.

Nanoeconomics is the economic theory of individual entity (human or device) predicted behavioral and performance propensities.

Schmarzo's Economic Digital Asset Valuation Theorem highlights how organizations can reduce marginal costs, increase marginal revenues, and accelerate value creation by sharing, reusing, and continuously refining the organization's data and analytic assets.

Sunk Cost Fallacy entails continuing to invest in a losing or failing venture because you've already invested a significant amount of time, money, or other resources you can't get back.

A Use Case is a cluster or aggregation of decisions around a common **Key Performance Indicator (KPI)** in support of specific business initiatives with quantifiable business or operational value.

A Value Engineering Framework decomposes the organization's strategic business initiative into its supporting business components (stakeholders, use cases, decisions, and KPIs) and data and analytics requirements.

Design thinking

A/B Testing is a user experience research methodology. A/B tests consist of a randomized experiment that usually involves two variants, although the concept can also be extended to multiple variants of the same variable.

Customer Co-Creation incorporates techniques that allow designers and developers to engage customers while generating and developing new business ideas of mutual interest. They are among the most value-enhancing, risk-reducing approaches to growth and innovation.

A Design Canvas is a template for consolidating a holistic gathering of the user or business requirements to ensure a relevant and meaningful outcome.

Journey Mapping is an ethnographic research method that traces the customer's *journey* as they interact with an organization while receiving a service, with particular attention to emotional highs and lows.

Experience Mapping is used to identify needs that customers are often unable to articulate.

Mind Mapping represents how ideas or other items are linked to a central idea and each other. Mind maps generate, visualize, structure, and classify ideas to look for patterns and insights that provide vital design criteria.

A Persona is an archetype of a user that helps designers and developers empathize with their users by understanding their business and personal contexts. Archetypes describe patterns of behaviors, attitudes, and motivations shared between people.

A Prioritization Matrix facilitates collaboration between business and data science stakeholders in identifying use cases with meaningful business value and practical feasibility of successful implementation.

Prototyping techniques seek to make abstract new ideas tangible through storyboarding, user scenarios, journeys, and business concept illustrations. These tools require deep collaboration with critical stakeholders to ideate, validate, and prioritize.

Rapid Prototyping techniques allow us to make abstract new ideas tangible to potential partners and customers. These include storyboarding, user scenarios, experience journeys, and business concept illustrations—all of which encourage deep involvement by essential stakeholders to provide feedback.

Storytelling is exactly how it sounds: weaving together a story rather than just making a series of points. It is a close relative of visualization—another way to make new ideas feel authentic and compelling. Visual storytelling is the most persuasive type of story. All good presentations—whether analytical or design-oriented—tell a compelling story.

A Storyboard is a graphic organizer with illustrations or images displayed sequentially for pre-visualizing a user (persona) interaction and engagement workflow.

Visualization leverages images or graphics to help users envision and validate the users' operational requirements and visualize their interactions with the operational system or application.

Data science and analytics

Artificial Intelligence (AI) is the simulation of human intelligence in machines programmed to think like humans and mimic their actions. The term may also be applied to any machine that exhibits traits associated with a human mind, such as learning and problem-solving.

Analytic Profiles codify, share, reuse, and continuously refine the predicted propensities, patterns, trends, and relationships for the organization's critical human and device assets or entities.

Analytic Scores are the results of analytical models factoring multiple variables and features to predict the likelihood of a behavior or action expressed as a single number. They are typically indexed from 0 to 100, where 100 indicates the highest confidence level in a behavior or an action. For example, a credit score predicts a person's likelihood of repaying their loan.

An AI Utility Function comprises the variables and metrics—and their associated weights— against which the AI model will seek to optimize as the basis for its decisions and actions to achieve the stated outcome. An AI model's preferences over possible actions can be defined by a function that maps these outcomes to a utility value; the higher the value, the more the AI model likes that action.

Classification and Clustering comprise the ability to identify clusters in data or classify objects into different categories. Classification uses predefined classes to which entities are assigned, whereas clustering identifies similarities between objects and groups according to shared characteristics.

Computer Vision (CV) is the ability to interpret and understand the visual world by identifying and classifying objects through images and video. The technology mimics human vision tasks, such as recognizing faces.

A Data Model is an abstract model that organizes elements of data and standardizes how they relate to one another and the properties of real-world entities.

Data Science is about identifying those variables and metrics that might be better predictors of behavior or performance. Data science is an interdisciplinary academic field that blends statistics, scientific methods, data management processes, and analytics to extract or extrapolate knowledge and insights from structured and unstructured data.

Deep Learning (Neural Networks) is based on artificial neural networks in which multiple processing layers extract progressively higher-level features from data.

IoT Edge refers to the **Internet of Things (IoT)** computing infrastructure that allows data processing and analysis to happen at the point where the data is generated.

Generative AI is an artificial intelligence system capable of generating text, images, or other media responding to a user's prompt or request.

Key Performance Indicators (**KPIs**) are quantifiable measures used to evaluate an organization's progress and ultimate success in achieving its business or operational objectives and goals.

A Large Language Model, or LLM, is a generative AI algorithm that can recognize, summarize, translate, predict, and generate text and other content based on knowledge gained from massive data sets.

ML Features are the mathematically transformed variables that AI/ML models use during training and inferencing to make predictions and guide actions or decisions.

Natural Language Processing (**NLP**) is the ability to understand or generate human language through human conversation or from documents. This entails applying algorithms that enable the conversion of speech into a form that computers can understand.

Predictions refer to the output of an algorithm after it has been trained on a historical data set and applied to new data when forecasting the likelihood of a particular outcome, such as whether a customer will churn in 30 days.

Propensity is the likelihood or predisposition of a person (or thing) to act or think in a particular way based on inherent qualities or past experiences or characteristics.

Recommendations are driven by an AI/ML algorithm to suggest a "next best action" or specific content based on historical data and what others "similar" to the user have done in a similar situation.

Reinforcement Learning is a machine learning training method that continuously learns and adapts to reward desired behaviors and punish undesired ones. Generally, a reinforcement learning agent can perceive and interpret its environment, take actions, and learn through trial and error.

Robotic process automation (**RPA**) is a software technology that makes it easy to build, deploy, and manage software robots that emulate human actions interacting with digital capabilities.

Schema on Load refers to pre-building a data schema before loading and subsequently querying the data in the data model.

Schema on Read refers to building a data schema on the fly as the query is being executed on the data model instead of needing to pre-build the schema (schema on load).

Simulation is the ability to model elements of the natural world to determine current and future outcomes and impacts of different scenarios and produce forecasts and predictions.

Speech Recognition recognizes and converts human speech into words or patterns that can be digitally stored and analyzed.

Supervised Machine Learning is a machine learning paradigm for problems where the available data consists of labeled examples, meaning that each data point contains features and an associated label.

The Thinking Like a Data Scientist methodology is a collaborative ideation, value-centric, human-empowered *scientific method* that seeks to unleash the predictive intuition of subject-matter experts in applying AI/ML to deliver relevant, meaningful, and ethical business and operational outcomes.

Unsupervised Machine Learning is an algorithm that analyzes, learns, and clusters patterns from untagged or unlabeled data sets.

packt.com

Subscribe to our online digital library for full access to over 7,000 books and videos, as well as industry leading tools to help you plan your personal development and advance your career. For more information, please visit our website.

Why subscribe?

- Spend less time learning and more time coding with practical eBooks and Videos from over 4,000 industry professionals
- Improve your learning with Skill Plans built especially for you
- Get a free eBook or video every month
- Fully searchable for easy access to vital information
- Copy and paste, print, and bookmark content

At www.packt.com, you can also read a collection of free technical articles, sign up for a range of free newsletters, and receive exclusive discounts and offers on Packt books and eBooks.

Other Books You May Enjoy

If you enjoyed this book, you may be interested in these other books by Packt:

The Economics of Data, Analytics, and Digital Transformation

Bill Schmarzo

ISBN: 9781800561410

- Train your organization to transition from being data-driven to being value-driven
- Navigate and master the big data business model maturity index
- Learn a methodology for determining the economic value of your data and analytics
- Understand how AI and machine learning can create analytics assets that appreciate in value the more that they are used
- Become aware of digital transformation misconceptions and pitfalls
- Create empowered and dynamic teams that fuel your organization's digital transformation

Machine Learning with PyTorch and Scikit-Learn

Sebastian Raschka

Yuxi (Hayden) Liu

Vahid Mirjalili

ISBN: 9781801819312

- Explore frameworks, models, and techniques for machines to learn from data
- Use scikit-learn for machine learning and PyTorch for deep learning
- Train machine learning classifiers on images, text, and more
- Build and train neural networks, transformers, and boosting algorithms
- Discover best practices for evaluating and tuning models
- Predict continuous target outcomes using regression analysis
- Dig deeper into textual and social media data using sentiment analysis

Packt is searching for authors like you

If you're interested in becoming an author for Packt, please visit authors.packtpub.com and apply today. We have worked with thousands of developers and tech professionals, just like you, to help them share their insight with the global tech community. You can make a general application, apply for a specific hot topic that we are recruiting an author for, or submit your own idea.

Share your thoughts

Now you've finished *AI & Data Literacy*, we'd love to hear your thoughts! Scan the QR code below to go straight to the Amazon review page for this book and share your feedback or leave a review on the site that you purchased it from.

https://packt.link/r/1835083501

Your review is important to us and the tech community and will help us make sure we're delivering excellent quality content.

Index

Download a free PDF copy of this book

Thanks for purchasing this book!

Do you like to read on the go but are unable to carry your print books everywhere? Is your eBook purchase not compatible with the device of your choice?

Don't worry, now with every Packt book you get a DRM-free PDF version of that book at no cost.

Read anywhere, any place, on any device. Search, copy, and paste code from your favorite technical books directly into your application.

The perks don't stop there, you can get exclusive access to discounts, newsletters, and great free content in your inbox daily

Follow these simple steps to get the benefits:

1. Scan the QR code or visit the link below

https://packt.link/free-ebook/9781835083505

2. Submit your proof of purchase
3. That's it! We'll send your free PDF and other benefits to your email directly